Carving Techniques

Madonna and Child by Henry Moore. Carved
in Hornton Stone. Church of St Matthew,
Northampton

Carving Techniques

Glynis Beecroft

Drawings and photographs by Edwin Beecroft

WATSON-GUPTILL PUBLICATIONS
NEW YORK

To my parents

For the American reader please note that

G-cramp = C-clamp
glasspaper = sandpaper
lolly stick = popsicle stick
plastercine = Plastalene
vice = vise

First published in the United States in 1976
by Watson-Guptill Publications,
a division of Billboard Publications, Inc.,
One Astor Plaza, New York, New York 10036

Copyright © 1976 by Glynis Beecroft
First published in 1976 in Great Britain
Reprinted 1977

Manufactured in Great Britain

Library of Congress Cataloging in Publication Data

Beecroft, Glynis.
    Carving techniques.
    Includes index.
    1. Sculpture-Technique. 2. Carving (Art industries) I. Title.
NB1170.B43   731.4'6   75–46629
ISBN 0–8230–0568–2

Contents

Acknowledgment

I should like to thank the following firms for their assistance in the preparation of this book: Ronald Adams Associates, E J Arnold and Son Limited, The Baxenden Chemical Company Limited, Black and Decker Limited, G H Bloore Limited, Candle Makers Supplies; The Boots Company Limited, The Brick Development Association, British Gypsum Limited, Durox Building Units Limited, Devcon Limited, Imperial Chemical Industries Limited, Ingram Thompson and Sons Limited, Petersfield Limeworks, Polycell Holdings Limited, Shearman and Company Limited, Stanley Tools Limited, Stone Industries, Thermalite Limited, Alec Tiranti Limited, The White Sea Baltic Company Limited.

I should also like to thank the following for their professional advice and assistance: Clive Nethercott for carving the stages and taking most of the photographs in the chapter on wood; Ingrid Atkinson for the section on wedging clay and for providing me with some of the examples of work in clay; Alan Saunders, of Bishop Otter College, Chichester, for finding examples of wood carvings by students; W J Crouch, Headmaster of Meadowlands County Junior School, for allowing me to work with groups of children at his school. I am grateful to Thelma M Nye for her sound advice during the production of this book.

Most especially I am indebted to my husband Edwin Beecroft, for doing the drawings and the majority of the photographs, as well as for his invaluable advice and encouragement during the writing of the book.

GMB

Unless otherwise stated, all the carved examples illustrated were made by the author for the book.

Introduction

Carving is often thought to be an activity requiring strength and stamina. This is a mistake. In fact, there are many different carving materials, some soft enough to be carved with a knife or spoon, others so hard that they need specially hardened tools to carve them.

I have deliberately chosen a wide range of materials. The softest materials – salt, soap, balsa wood, clay, wax and polyurethane – require no specialised equipment, and can be carved by both young and old. Reflecting the growing interest in sculpture at school level, I have included a few notes on new materials, some of which may be directly carved using simple tools, and some of which are self-hardening compounds allowing preliminary shaping before carving. The hardest materials to carve are stone and wood, but even these vary tremendously in the degree of hardness and softness. Generally, however, they need to be carved with hammer and chisels and require that the beginner master the skill of using them in order to carve a sculpture. For this reason, what may be called the traditional tools and techniques of carving are dealt with in some detail. Some knowledge of these tools and techniques will be of advantage in carving the range of materials of medium hardness – chalk, plaster, building blocks, bricks and acrylic plastic – which are well within the scope of both adults and children. Obviously the approach will be different. A child might find a large building block intimidating until it is sawn into smaller pieces, which can then be held in the hand and carved with blunt knives or spoons. The same is true of chalk or plaster. Some of the most sophisticated sculpture is made in plaster before being cast into bronze. Yet a small block that has been formed by pouring liquid plaster into a yogurt cup will carve easily into a little figure using only files and glasspaper.

Carving, taken at any level, can offer a great deal. Children enjoy making things. Carving gives them an opportunity to build up confidence in using tools in a purposeful way. It also helps them to understand the three-dimensional world. A child who has removed the corners and edges of a cube to change it into a sphere has discovered for itself something about the nature of squareness and roundness. For adults, what could make a more worthwhile pursuit than one which combines gentle exercise and fresh air with the great satisfaction that comes from turning a rough block of material into a finished sculpture, using the simplest of traditional tools? Perfect! . . . but then I'm biased.

GMB 1976

Safety precautions
Care must of course be taken at all times when using sharp implements but a knowledge of how to use them correctly reduces considerably any risk.

Introducing carving

The process of carving

Carving is the process of sawing, chipping or scraping a block of material such as stone or wood to remove unwanted pieces until the block takes on the form that the sculptor has in mind.

Sculpture starts in the mind. The sculptor has an idea which he wants to realize in sculptural form.

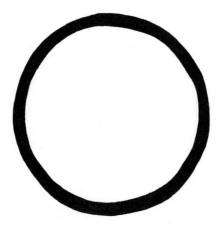

Diagrammatic form of sculptural idea

The sculptor next selects his material. He chooses a block from which he can carve his sculpture with the minimum of hard work and wastage.

Diagrammatic form of block

There are three main groups of tools which the sculptor may need when carving hard materials.

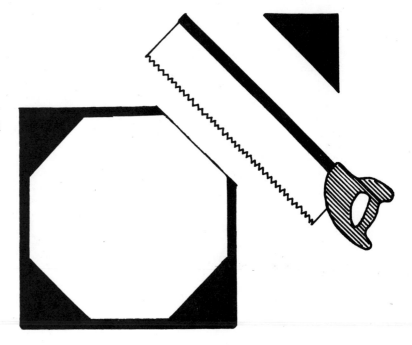

Saws can be used to make an initial series of cuts. The sculpture will then have a 'blocked out' appearance

A hammer and chisel may be used to take the sculpture from the blocked out stage to a stage of near completion

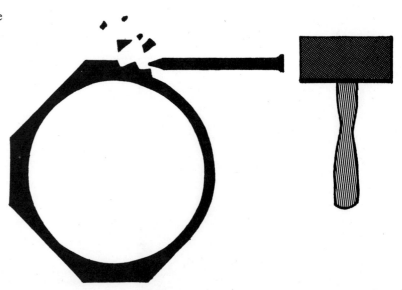

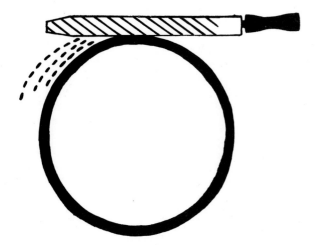

With a variety of abrasives such as rasps, files
or glasspapers, the sculpture may be given the
required degree of finish

Sculptures in softer materials, such as salt,
soap, wax or clay, progress through the same
stages, though the tools used are different.
With soap, for example, a knife may be used
for blocking out (using a deep, cutting action),
for carving detail (using the point of the knife
to make incisive cuts), and for smoothing the
surface (using the edge of the knife with a
scraping action).

Thinking in three dimensions

So far, the sculptural idea has been thought of
only in a two-dimensional way. The sculptor
must learn to think 'in the round'. To go back
to our diagrammatic form (page 9), this now
needs to be thought of as a solid object, a
sphere – like a football. The sphere is an easy
three-dimensional form to understand, because
its contours are regular. In other words, it's the
same at the back as it is at the front. But most
forms used in sculpture are more complicated
than this. It is not always evident when
working on the front of a carving just what
form the sides and back should take. Such
knowledge comes mainly from experience, and
from having a 'feel' for sculpture. But this
process of thinking in three dimensions can be
helped in a number of ways.

1 By drawing objects from different points of
   view.
2 By making collections of natural and man-
   made objects which by accident look like
   ready-made sculptures. Objects like this can
   be seen all around us in the form of mis-
   shapen fruit and vegetables, pebbles and
   rocks, driftwood and gnarled branches and
   roots, broken pieces of furniture, discarded
   machine parts, twisted pieces of metal, and
   so on.
3 By looking at sculpture in museums and art
   galleries. The beginner should not restrict
   himself to a single theme, but should try to
   see as wide a range of sculpture as possible.
   Work by lesser known or local artists is often
   more encouraging for the beginner, who
   might well be discouraged from starting if his
   only contact with carving has been with
   plaster copies of the Old Masters.
4 By actually making sculpture. In a practical
   subject like carving, learning by doing is
   vital. But there is no point in making the
   subject needlessly difficult. The beginner
   should start with the softer materials, so that
   he can make changes to the form quickly and
   easily. After all, the principles of carving are
   the same whether you work in butter or in
   granite.

Working in three dimensions

The general principles of carving have already been sketched in the introduction. Difficulties arise in knowing how to start. A neatly-sawn block of wood or stone may be daunting. It can be a good idea to start with a less regularly-shaped block which gives the appearance of already having been carved to a certain extent. This eliminates the difficult and often tedious job of blocking out the preliminary shape of the sculpture. The sculptor may select such a block to fit an idea he already has, or he may allow the shape of the block to suggest an idea to him. Some random lumps are so close to being ready-made sculptures that they need the minimum of working to complete them.

Log suggesting an animal form

The finished sculpture is produced simply by refinement of the existing form

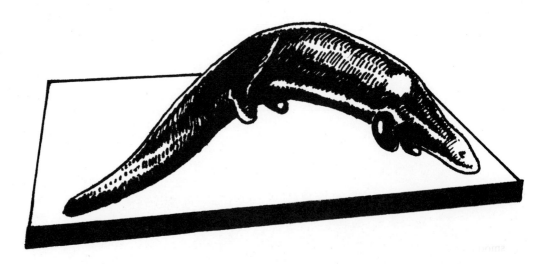

Of course, not all random lumps provide such ready-made sculptures. In some cases they suggest only the beginning of an idea, and a lot of unwanted material will have to be removed to complete the carving. This way of working is further described in the section on carving a lump of soapstone on page 23. When the block to be carved is simply a cube, giving little or no help in suggesting the finished form of the work, the sculptor may need to block out the rough form for himself. Blocking out is the process of removing the unwanted masses of the sculpture in large blocks. It serves two purposes. By removing large pieces quickly and efficiently, it saves the sculptor a lot of unnecessarily hard work. At the same time, it

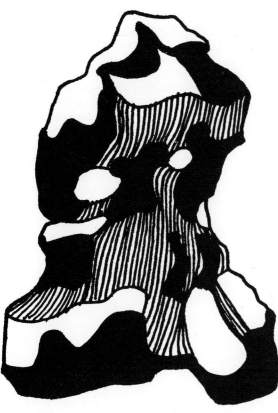

Random lump of stone suggesting a human form

The sculpture is completed by rounding and smoothing the form

Original cube-shaped block

reveals the basic form of the sculpture, though in a somewhat 'geometrical' way. The tools for blocking out are those which produce straight cuts. These may be knives, in the case of soft materials like soap and wax, or saws for the harder materials. If a particularly hard stone is to be blocked out, it may sometimes be necessary to take it to a stone mason. Some beginners find it helpful to approach the subject of blocking out through a series of basic exercises in which they try to carve some simple solids from the original cube. Some regular solids are the cylinder, the pyramid, the cone and the sphere.

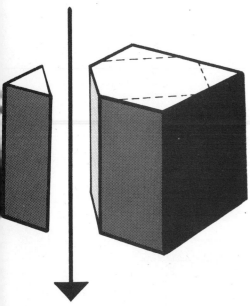

Cut vertically through each corner

Blocked out form
and
Final form after smoothing

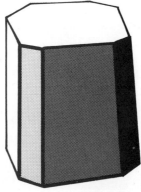

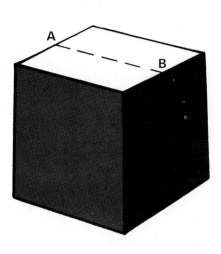

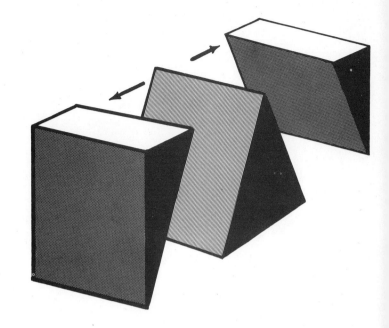

Original cube. The cutting tool is placed on the line A–B and cuts diagonally towards the lower edges of the cube

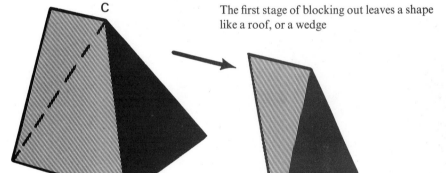

The first stage of blocking out leaves a shape like a roof, or a wedge

In the second stage, the cutting tool is placed on the mid-point, C, and diagonal cuts are again made to the lower edges

The final form is a four-sided pyramid

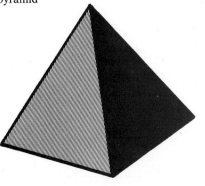

If the edges of the pyramid are filed away and smoothed off, the resulting form is a cone

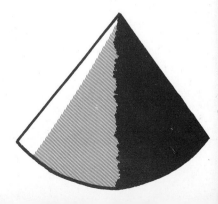

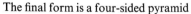

Original cube

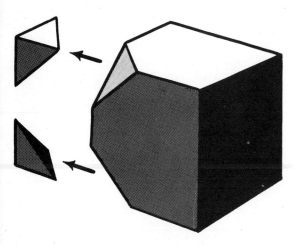

The eight corners are removed, using diagonal cuts

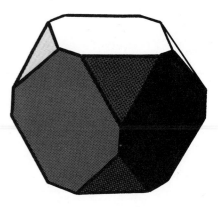

Blocked out form

Final form after smoothing

For the beginner, the process of carving more complicated forms may be helped by seeing them in terms of simpler forms such as these. A human head and neck, for example, may be thought of as a spherical or egg-shaped form resting on a cylinder.

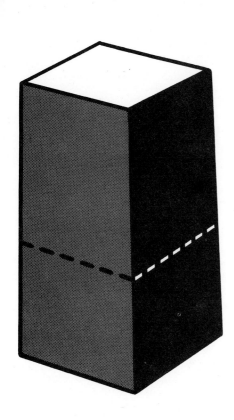

Original block
The dotted lines divide the block into head and
neck areas

The neck is roughly blocked out

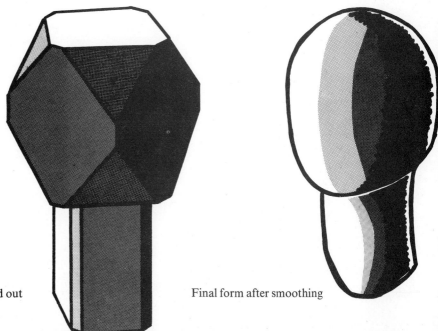

The head and neck are further blocked out

Final form after smoothing

Individual features are given their position by drawing on the surface of the block. Some sculptors do very detailed drawings on all sides of the block, including top and bottom, and follow this with a blocking out plan, using hatching to indicate areas to be removed. A block prepared in this way might look like this:

Working in this way, the sculptor knows exactly how much of the material he can afford to remove. Chiselling – or gouging and paring away in the case of a soft material – will reveal further details of individual features, and at the same time will alter the character of the form away from the original over-simplified appearance. In the course of the chiselling stage, a good deal of the original drawing is often removed. This the sculptor replaces when and where it is required. When carving from random lumps, it is often quite impossible to do detailed drawings, at least until the surface has had some of its roughness carved away.

Subject matter

Human and animal forms have been the traditional subject matter of sculpture for many thousands of years. The wide variety of animal form, and the almost unlimited range of expressive shapes the human form can adopt, have provided the sculptor with an endless supply of inspiration. One has only to observe, in buses, trains, cafés and other public places, the vast differences in the way people sit or stand, to realise why sculptors have found the human form so absorbing. Then there is the wide range of expressive states which may be conveyed through the human form. A pose may express joy, sadness, anger, frustration, tenderness, strength, fragility, grace – the list is almost endless. Groups of figures can be used to express a single theme, or a juxtaposition of more than one theme. It is only in recent times that sculptors have felt the need to expand their subject matter to include non-figurative forms.

Holding work steady

Some sculpture, due to its weight or proportions, is capable of being carved without the necessity of holding it steady. But there is nothing quite so annoying as trying to carve a block of stone which keeps jumping away with each chisel blow. There are several ways of holding work in position.

The professional way to hold wood is by means of a bench screw. This is an object like a long thin bolt with a pointed end in the form of a screw. It passes through a hole in the bench into the wood and is tightened by means of a butterfly nut. Alternatively, large screws may be used to attach the work to a wooden base, which can then be clamped to the bench. When carving stone, a strong bolt may be cemented in a hole in the bottom of the work. The bolt is passed through a hole in the bench, and secured by means of a nut and washer. Vices and clamps are another means of holding work steady. Materials strong enough to withstand chisel blows can be held in wood vices. The jaws may need to be lined with strips of leather or felt, in order to protect the work. G-cramps or C-clamps as they are called in the USA, can be used, but they get in the way of the chisel, and have a tendency to slip on rounded surfaces.

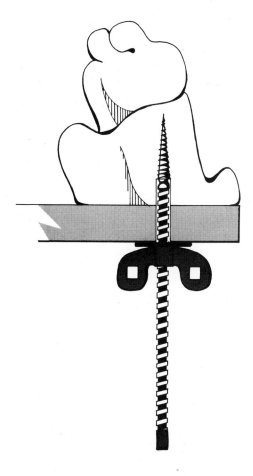

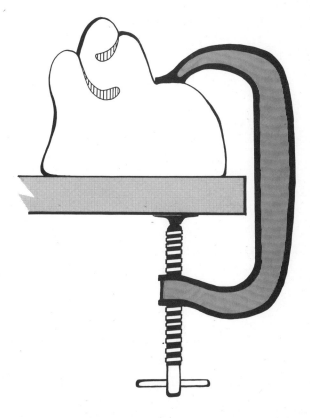

Different methods of holding work steady

Finally, there are several methods which do not require specialised equipment. Some of the softer materials need only be held in the hand. Four lengths of wood may be nailed or screwed to the bench so that the sculpture fits inside them and is held securely. Small sculpture can be held reasonably well by making a wooden box (an old orange box would do) and filling it with sand. The sculpture can then be pressed into the sand deep enough to hold it steady.

Bases

Sculpture may be displayed free-standing or mounted on a base. Bases have a number of functions. They serve to 'set off' the sculpture, giving it a finished appearance. They may raise a sculpture to a better viewing position. They may also support in an upright position work which cannot balance by itself. Wood and stone are the traditional and most useful materials for making bases. The sculpture can be displayed on the base without being attached to it, or it can be glued or screwed in position. Small, light work may be stuck with any high strength glue. Wood sculpture can be attached with long screws which pass through the base and straight into the wood. Heavier work in stone requires a hole drilled into the stone and a bolt set into the hole with a strong cement or glue. A hole also needs to be drilled through the base and countersunk so that the bolt can be tightened with a nut and washer. Stone bases are generally ordered from a stone mason, who will cut them to the precise measurements required. Make certain, if he has to drill a hole, that your measurements for it are very accurate. To get the right proportions for the base it is a good idea to cut a square of card and place it under the sculpture to see if the area of the base looks correct.

Wooden bases can be made quite easily. Try to use a piece of wood that has been planed, so that once the base has been cut to shape it only requires finishing with a coarse, medium and then a fine glasspaper. Any of the treatments given in the chapter on wood are suitable (see page 94) and depend on whether the sculptor wants a base with a high shine or matt finish. If the sculpture is to be stuck to a base that has already been varnished, the area to be glued must first be roughened with glasspaper. Sculpture will not adhere to a wooden base which has been treated with an oil preparation. To get good adhesion, the shape of the base of the sculpture should be traced on the wood, and this area should be left untreated when the rest of the wood is oiled. Finally, if the work is to be displayed indoors, a piece of felt should be stuck to the bottom of the base to prevent damage to furniture. Rolls of self-adhesive felt can be bought for this purpose from hardware shops.

Salt

Children from the earliest age enjoy the process of carving a shape from a block. Many of the carving materials are unsuitable because they require the use of sharp tools. Salt is one of the easiest to carve for this age group – although this should not prevent adults from experimenting with the material. Salt can be easily carved with a blunt knife or spoon. Pieces of wood, lolly sticks or even rubbing with the hands will work equally well. Salt does not keep very long, as the dampness in the atmosphere causes it to crumble. Kept in a dry place it should last for several months.

Obtaining salt
Few supermarkets stock block salt now, so it is better to try a small grocer or delicatessen. Some cash and carry shops stock the salt blocks but it is usually necessary to buy them in bulk, ie a dozen or more blocks. Where difficulties are met in obtaining salt, enquiries may be made to Ingram and Sons Ltd, Lion Salt Works, Marston, Nr Northwich, Cheshire, who will be able to supply the name of the nearest stockist. In the USA block salt is sold in the form of 'salt licks' or 'salt block' for livestock and may be obtained at farming supply outlets or agriculture and farm supply chains. City-dwellers might look in their local Yellow Pages under 'Feed Dealers'.

Block of salt, salt sculptures, knife and spoon for carving

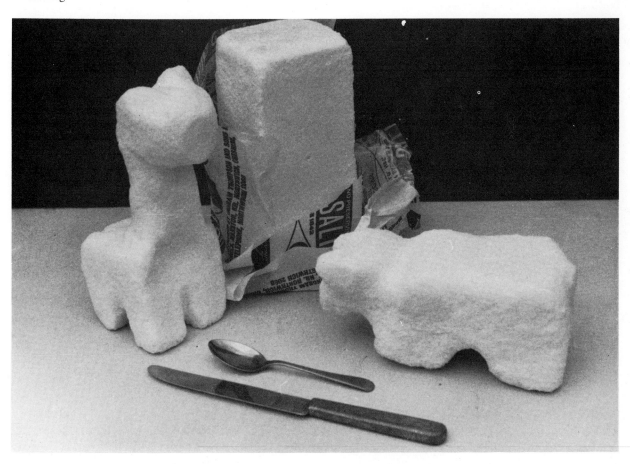

22

Tools and equipment
Any of the following:
   Spoons or old knife
   Clean sheet of polythene (polyethylene) on
   which to work
   Lolly sticks
   Flat pieces of wood
     Providing the salt is carved in clean
conditions it can be used afterwards for
cooking.

Technique
The only way to carve salt is by scraping the
surface of the salt block. It is not a good idea to
cut away large pieces at a time in case the block
breaks. By slowly crumbling away unwanted
areas the shape is achieved. Try to choose
simple shapes to carve, as salt is not compact
enough for detailed forms.

Finishes
Salt must be left in its natural state. The drier
the atmosphere, the longer it will keep.

A 4-year old carving a giraffe in salt

Soap

Soap is an interesting medium to carve. Sculptors used sometimes to practice on some detail for a portrait sculpture using a piece of soap. When they were sure that they had got it right they would proceed to carve the detail into stone. Soap is another medium ideally suited to young children, because of the ease with which it can be carved using the simplest of tools. Soap is a little more permanent than salt but once it dries out it loses its soft, plastic appearance.

Obtaining blocks of soap

These days, it is very difficult to obtain soap in large blocks. None of the leading soap manufacturers makes anything very much bigger than a bath size. Some schools, hospitals and similar institutions still use the large blocks which they cut up into smaller pieces. Large blocks of washing soap can sometimes be bought, but even with these the tendency now is to cut them in half before packaging them. It is therefore necessary to restrict work to a smaller scale. Soap can be bought in a wide range of makes and colours from any general shop or chemist. White washing soap is a good consistency to carve. Some of the transparent soaps are interesting to carve, though rather brittle. Glycerine soap, a semi-transparent, amber-coloured soap normally used for cleaning leather, is good for carving. It is sold in a good sized block, but is rather expensive. It is obtained from saddlers or shops selling leather goods.

Tools and equipment

Any of the following:
   Nail files
   Knives
   Spatulas
   Potato peelers
   Damp rag for smoothing and polishing

Tools for carving soap

Technique

The approach to carving soap is straightforward. The process is one of peeling away the soap until arriving at the finished shape. The surface can be made smooth by rubbing a damp cloth over it. Should any pieces break off, they can be cemented back by wetting both surfaces and pressing firmly together. They can be pegged with cocktail sticks or toothpicks to make them even more secure. This method is sometimes successful for pressing the blocks together to make a larger one for carving. Textures can be made in the soap with the use of serrated-edged and pointed instruments. Flakes of soap can be cemented back by wetting them, to add another type of texture.

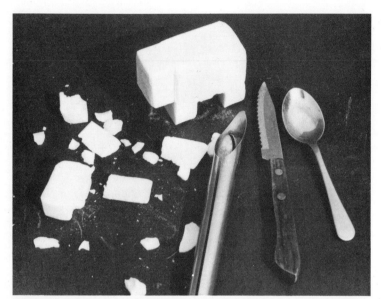

Stages in carving a sheep in soap

The bar of washing soap has been blocked out with a knife

The forms have been roughly rounded, using a knife and potato peeler

Finished carving

Finishes

The disadvantage of soap is that it dries up
fairly quickly and loses its waxy appearance.
Several coats of clear varnish will help to
prevent this. Alternatively, when it begins to
dry up it can be used for washing.

Soap carvings in washing soap and carbolic
soap by children from Purbrook County
Grammar School, Hampshire

Balsa wood

Balsa is one of the softest woods for carving. It is widely used in schools because of the ease with which it can be worked. It makes an ideal medium for young children and beginners, and can be carved using the minimum of equipment.

Obtaining balsa wood

Most toy, hobby and art shops sell balsa wood, although it is more usual for them to stock the strips used for model-making rather than blocks that can be carved. If local stockists are unable to order blocks, they can be ordered in packs from most of the leading suppliers of art materials to schools. When ordering, it is important to state the type of balsa wood required. Packs generally contain all blocks, all strips or a mixture of both.

Tools and equipment

Tenon saw or hacksaw
Any sharp blade – craft knives, kitchen knives, etc
Files, Surforms
Glasspaper
Note: it is possible to carve balsa wood using only files or Surforms.

Pack of balsa wood

Technique
Stages in carving a simple animal form in balsa
wood

Areas to be removed drawn on to block of
balsa wood

Unwanted areas cut away with a saw

Sculpture shaped with the use of files, Surforms and a craft knife

Completed sculpture of a rabbit. Beads have been stuck on for the eyes, and bristles from a broom for the whiskers. An application of wood stain and a coat of varnish was used for the final finish. This carving was made by a 9 year old girl at Meadowlands County Junior School, Hampshire

Animal sculptures by 8–10 year old children
from Meadowlands County Junior School,
Hampshire. Most of these were made using
only junior hacksaws and Surforms

**Stages in carving a more complex form in balsa
wood**
A more sophisticated approach to carving
balsa wood can be achieved by a whittling
technique with knives or chisels. Far more
detail can be obtained using this method of
carving.

Outline for sculpture drawn on to block. The black areas were then removed, using a small saw

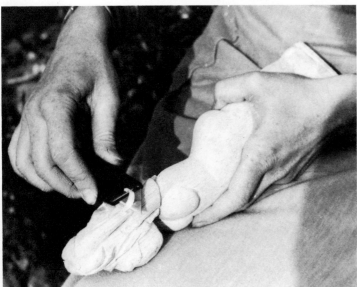

Fine details were achieved by paring off thin slivers of balsa wood, using a sharp craft knife

The figure was finished by smoothing with glasspaper

Balsa wood carving by Edwin Beecroft

Finishes
Balsa wood will take the same colour treatments as any other wood. It can be painted, stained or varnished. (See page 94)

Clay

Where space and tools are limited, clay can be used with the minimum of equipment. An old spoon or knife will do as well as any sophisticated carving tools. Clay, unlike any other carving medium, has the great advantage that it can be worked in its wet or dry state and any of the stages in between. When wet it is soft and malleable, when dry it is hard and brittle. This means that in its wet state it can be squeezed into shape, when 'leather hard' (the consistency of cheese) it can be carved and scraped, and when dry it can be glasspapered to a smooth finish. A further advantage is that carving clay is not as final as carving most materials. When mistakes are made, or where radical alterations need to be made to the

Leather hard clay is clean enough to be worked indoors

sculpture, the clay can be damped down again and remodelled. Clay is one of the most versatile of sculpture materials and although more usually modelled in its wet form its suitability as a carving medium should not be underestimated. Those who have only used it in its soft state will be surprised at the different effects that can be achieved by using it when leather hard. The ease with which it can be carved and its relative cleanness in this dry state makes it a most pleasurable material to work with.

The only disadvantage of clay is that in order to preserve the finished article it needs to be fired in a kiln. This heats it to a very high temperature, which then makes it durable and permanent. Problems of firing work can sometimes be overcome by approaching a local pottery, school, college or further education pottery class. The cost of firing a small item can be minimal. For schools, some education authorities provide a service whereby the schoolchildren's clay work is collected, fired and returned to the school. It is also possible to fire work by building a sawdust kiln in the garden. This is usually done by digging a pit, or by building up bricks or using an old oil drum. It is important that the kiln is sited in an open position to prevent fire risk. It is then packed with sawdust and the work to be fired. The sawdust is ignited from the top and the slow smouldering produces, over a period of time, enough heat to fire the clay. Full details on the method for building a kiln, ventilating it, etc can be found in most of the more comprehensive books on pottery.

Obtaining clay

Work to be fired should be made from good quality clay, particularly if it is going to be fired in a kiln with other people's work. If there are impurities in the clay it is likely that the work will explode in the kiln and damage other work being fired. Clay to be fired should be bought from a reputable firm. Clay is usually sold in bags of 50 kilos. Art shops often sell smaller quantities. The colour of clay varies depending on the area that it comes from, but the two basic colours are terracotta and grey. There are a number of firms that supply clay and pottery equipment. (See page 138)

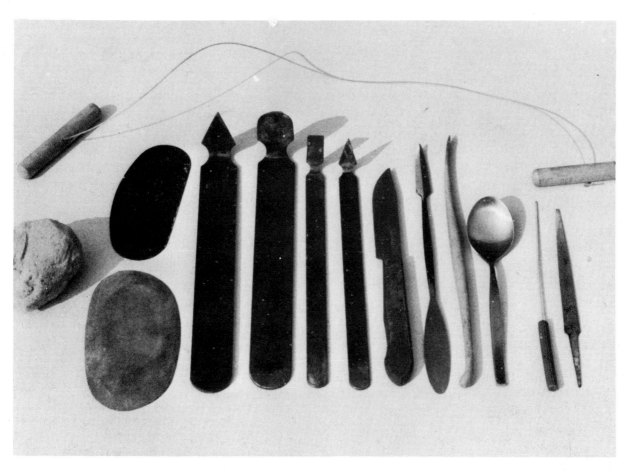

A selection of tools for gouging, scraping and
filing the clay. The tools include a wire with
toggles at each end for wedging, a sponge,
kidney scrapers, a kitchen knife, metal and
wood pottery tools, a spoon and small files

Tools and equipment
Table or bench
Polythene (polyethylene) to protect table
Any of the following
Sponge
Boxwood modelling tools
Knife
Spoon
Old dental tools
Spatula
Nail file
Files
Glasspaper

Technique
It is advisable to work with a piece of clay that
is no bigger than a football. Anything larger
increases the likelihood of the clay cracking
while it is drying out. It is advisable to carve
compact forms, as elongated shapes are likely
to crack during the drying out stage. If the clay
is to be fired it is necessary to 'wedge' it. This
process, rather like kneading bread, mixes the
clay to an even consistency and knocks out any
pockets of air. Wedging is best demonstrated
rather than described. The following
photographs show the stages of wedging. Like
any new process, learning the action of
wedging clay takes time and practice before the
different stages become a smooth, rhythmic
action.

Wedging Take a piece of clay about the size of a small football. Pat it into a roughly spherical shape and place it on a strong table or bench ready to start wedging.

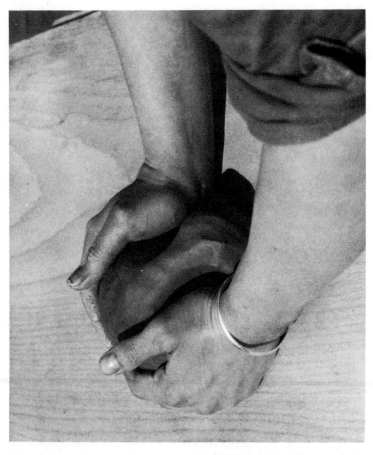

Place a hand on each side of the clay sphere and then press the heel of the hand downwards and inwards. Remove hands ready to start the next part of the action

Lift the shape upwards and towards the body and then press down again with a circular movement of the hands, and wrist. Repeat this process several times until the 'ram's head' shape is formed

Ram's head

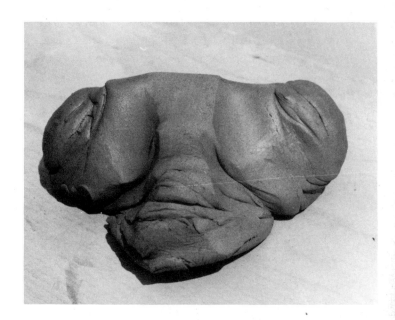

The clay has been cut in half to show how it is becoming mixed. To demonstrate this, the lump of clay was made up using two clays of different colour

Pat ram's head gently into a sphere

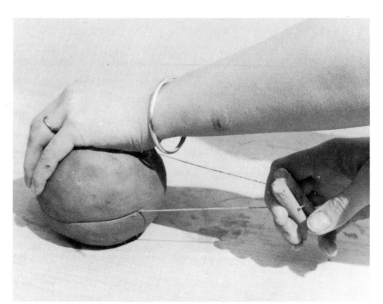

Cut sphere in half by pulling cheese wire through it towards the body in one gentle action

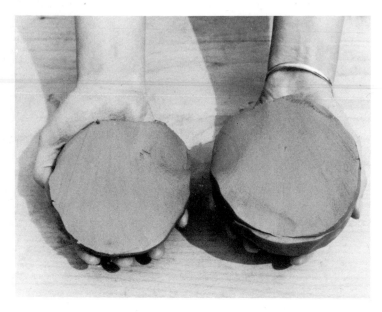

Study the two halves for air pockets and if there are any present repeat the wedging process. When there are no longer any air pockets present, smack the two halves together again and begin work

Forming the basis of a shape for carving Clay can be left in a lump and then carved. However, as it is a malleable material, it is worth taking advantage of this and forming it into a shape that sparks off an idea or approximates to an idea already formed in the mind. There are many ways of shaping the clay prior to carving. A few suggestions are given below:

Shaping the clay by slapping it down on to a flat surface

Shaping the clay by twisting it

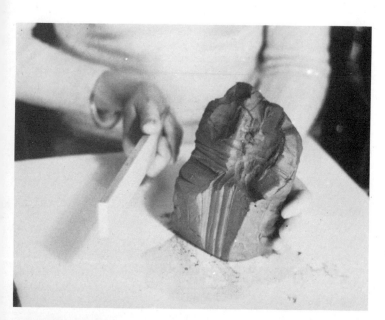

Shaping the clay by beating it with a flat stick

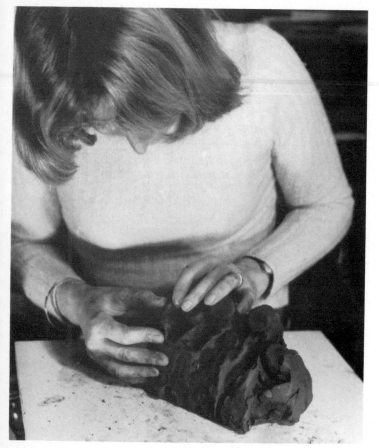

Shaping the clay by modelling with the fingers

The clay must then be put aside until it has dried leather hard (the consistency of soap). It is then ready to be carved. This is done by paring away the clay in thin slivers with a sharp tool

Paring away the clay with a knife

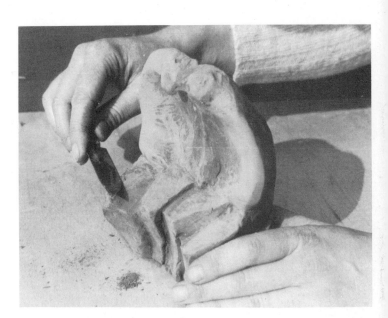

Gouging into the clay with a spoon

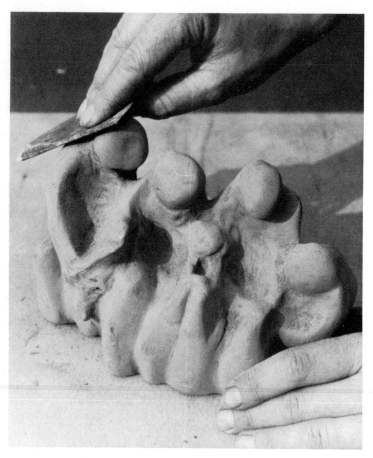

Rubbing the sculpture with a piece of
glasspaper will give the surface a smooth finish

If the work needs to be left until another day
it can be placed in a polythene bag and sealed
with a wire tag (the type used for bread
packaging or deep freezing). If the clay dries
out too much during the carving it should be
wrapped in a slightly damp cloth and sealed in
a polythene bag for several hours. When the
carving stage has been completed, work to be
fired must be hollowed out before the clay can
be left to dry. Ideally, no part of the sculpture
should be thicker than 13 mm ($\frac{1}{2}$ in). To help
prevent cracking during the drying out stage
the work should be put in a place of even
temperature out of any draughts. An airing
cupboard is ideal. This can take anything from
two days to several weeks, depending on the
volume of the clay and temperature of the
room. Should any cracks appear while the clay
is drying, it is necessary to wrap it in a damp
cloth and seal it in a polythene bag until the
clay becomes moist. The cracks can then be
pushed together by working with the fingers,
and the drying process started again.

When the clay has completely dried out it
should have lightened both in colour and
weight and it should have a dry dusty feel. The
dry clay can then be glasspapered to give it a
smooth finish.

Before firing in a kiln most potters like the
clay to have been drying out for some weeks. It
is wise at this stage to take the advice of the
person who is going to do the firing.

Finishes
Firing in a kiln is the traditional way of making clay permanent. During the firing process glaze can be applied to the surface of the clay to give it a colour. There are many different coloured glazes to choose from, depending on the range used by the pottery doing the firing. Sculpture in clay that has been fired is often referred to as 'ceramic'.

Making beads in clay

Three ceramics carved from cone shaped lumps of clay by Ingrid Atkinson

Three stages in the carving of a piggy bank by Ingrid Atkinson

Ceramic sculptures after glazing and firing

Carved ceramic jewellery by a group of 13–15 year old children

Three Figures by Pat Jackson

Saint John by Yvonne Hudson

Wax

Wax is one of the traditional modelling materials for making sculpture to be cast into bronze. Sculpture in wax is perfectly acceptable, providing it is handled carefully, exhibited indoors, and kept away from a direct source of heat. The material can be easily prepared and carved and the tools required for working are simple and readily available. Wax can be worked with the minimum of mess and wastage. Wax chippings can be collected together, melted down and re-used.

Obtaining wax

Wax for carving can be bought in the form of domestic candles, decorative candles or blocks of paraffin wax. Wax can also be bought in candle making kits. White domestic candles can be bought from any general shop.

Decorative candles can be bought from gift shops and department stores. Paraffin wax can be bought from some large chemists. It can also be bought from wax and candle makers suppliers.

Tools

Wax can be carved with an assortment of the following:
  Vegetable knives
  Penknives
  Boxwood modelling tools
  Dental instruments
  Lino cutting tools
  Fine steel wool
  Clean cloth and petrol or white spirit

Making and carving a block

The wax should be melted in a small saucepan or double burner over a very gentle heat. The wax may be coloured by the addition of coloured wax crayons or wax dye. Wax crayons are more suitable than dyes for colouring sculpture as they do not fade as quickly. The melted wax can be poured into moulds made from small cardboard boxes, tins, yogurt cups, etc. (Tins should be wetted before pouring in the wax.) When the wax has hardened it can be removed from the mould. Cardboard boxes may have to be soaked in water in order to peel them easily from the hardened wax. Metal moulds can be warmed slightly to melt the outer surface of the wax

block, which will then slip out of the mould. The waxy non-stick surface of the yogurt and polythene cups allows the hardened wax to be tapped out easily. Before carving, the design can be drawn on to the block with a pointed tool. Much of the rough shaping can be done with knives, while detail and modelling of rounded shapes can be achieved with fine bladed instruments, boxwood modelling tools, lino cutting tools and dental instruments. Surfaces can be smoothed and polished with a rag dipped in petrol or white spirit.

Tools and equipment for casting blocks of wax

  Moulds (yogurt cups, tins, boxes, polythene food containers, etc)
  Saucepan or double burner for melting wax
  Gas/electric cooker or ring for heating wax
  Thermometer (wax should not be heated above 135°–140°F, 56°–58°C)
  Microcrystalline wax (optional)
  Block of paraffin wax/bag of paraffin wax or white household candles
  Wax dye or wax crayons

Topping up

After the wax has been poured into the mould and cooled it will be found that the level has dropped, leaving a hollow. As soon as this occurs a little more wax should be heated in the saucepan and the level of the block topped up. Topping up should not be delayed, for if the wax becomes too hard the new layer is likely to separate during carving.

Moulds and waxes for casting a block of wax. The bag on the left contains paraffin wax in granulated form. This saves cutting up solid blocks of wax and it also melts more quickly. The solid block is paraffin wax. Pieces can be cut from the block with a sharp knife. Alternatively, white domestic candles, which are also made of paraffin wax, can be used. The bag in the centre contains pieces of microcrystalline wax which can be added in small quantities to the melted paraffin wax. The addition of this wax makes the block softer for carving, although it is not essential. Cardboard boxes, cups, etc. can be used for moulds. The thermometer is used to check that the wax is not overheated. Wax crayons or wax dyes can be added to the melted wax to colour it

Pouring melted wax into the mould

Carving the block with a craft knife. The block is being carved to make two joined cylinder shapes which will form the basis for two figures

The addition of detail and modelling to the two
cylinder shapes begins to make them
recognisable as two figures. Wood modelling
tools, small knives, lino tools, etc are all useful
for this stage

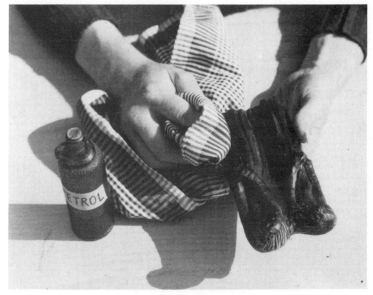

White spirit or petrol applied with a rag and
rubbed into the surface makes a smooth,
finished effect

48

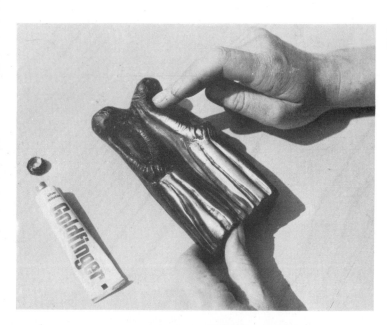

Goldfinger a metal coloured paste is applied lightly to the surface to highlight the detail

The finished sculpture – *Two Girls*. The surface can be painted or sprayed with clear lacquer to protect it and prevent the *Goldfinger* rubbing off. (For information on *Goldfinger* and similar products see section on finishes for plaster, page 116).

Carving candles

Candle making has become a popular hobby in the last few years, and carving into the surface of the candle offers an interesting way of taking the results one stage further. Carving candles is quite an art in itself and many exciting results can be achieved by experimenting.

There are two ways to approach candle carving. Either the candles can be made by buying the necessary materials, or candles can be bought ready-made from a gift shop. When buying candles for carving it is important to choose ones that are not too brittle and not the type with colour only on the outside. It is sometimes necessary to buy several and experiment.

Tools and equipment

The tools and equipment for casting candles are the same as for casting a block of wax. Any cylindrical container may be used as a mould. Polythene food containers, empty washing up liquid containers and yogurt cups are suitable. It is better to choose a container that can be thrown away, as ideally a hole needs to be pierced in the bottom through which the wick is threaded. Also, if there is any difficulty in removing the candle, the mould may be cut away. It is possible to buy candle moulds that have the hole for the wick and a dome shaped top that gives the candle a professional look. The following additional things are required for casting candles:

Wicks

Mould seal or plasticine
(to prevent the melted wax running out of the wick hole)

Candle making kits containing a comprehensive booklet of instructions, and everything that is required for making candles, can be bought from the suppliers given at the end of the book.

Technique for casting a candle

The basic method for casting a candle is explained below but it should be remembered that candle making is a subject in its own right. There are books available that deal with the art of candle making in detail.

Candle making kit

50

Shampoo, washing-up liquid or similar container. Pierce a small hole through the bottom of the mould, in the centre

Thread the wick through the hole so that it protrudes 15 mm ($\frac{5}{8}$ in)

Dip the protruding part of the wick in melted wax (this keeps the wick free of mould seal or plasticine which would prevent it lighting)

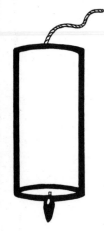

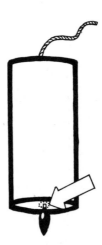

Press a little mould seal or plasticine round the hole to prevent wax leaking

Place a stick across top of container and tie wick to it. Make sure that the wick is in the middle of the mould

Pour in wax. Fill to brim. As the wax cools the
level falls. Top up with more wax

When quite cool tap mould to facilitate
removal of candle

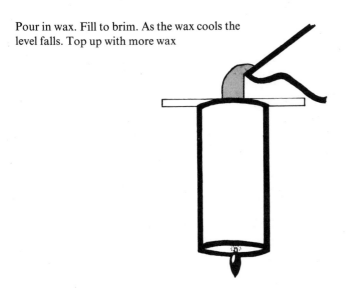

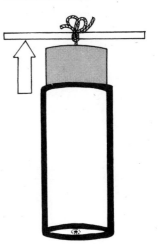

Cut off wick close to candle

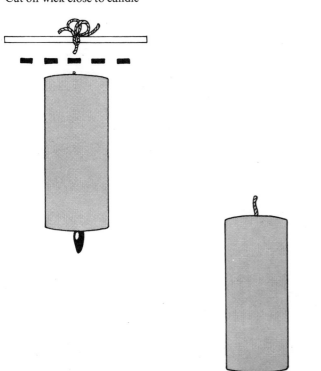

Turn candle upside down, so that end of wick
that was dipped in wax is now at the top

Carving candles

The design can be drawn directly on the wax
using a pointed instrument, such as a hat pin or
darning needle. Alternatively, paper cut-outs
can be stuck on the candle surface and the
outlines drawn using the same instruments.
Magazine illustrations or photographs can be
stuck to the candle and traced on to the surface
by pricking through the paper, which is then
peeled off, leaving the design as a series of dots.
Don't forget to leave a space at the bottom if
the candle is to be displayed in a candle holder.
The design can be cut away with any fine tool.
Be careful while carving that the heat from
your hands is not blurring the carved design. If
the candle does become too warm put it in the
fridge for a few minutes to harden the wax.

Stage in carving a candle cast from a washing-up liquid bottle. Strips of masking tape have been wrapped round the candle to break up the design into panels

The completed candle. The design is based on two rings of children holding hands

Finishes

The candle surface can be polished with the hands or a soft cloth. A rag with a little white spirit or petrol will smooth any roughness in the carving. Relief work can be highlighted by colouring the surface with water soluble paint such as acrylic mixed with a little soap. Paint the candle and rub off just before it dries, leaving colour in the crevices. Do not overdo this as water soluble paint will not burn and may clog the wick if used in excess. *Goldfinger* made by Rowney puts a metallic coloured finish on to the wax surface.

Foamed plastic

Expanded polystyrene and expanded polyurethane are two of the more recent man-made materials that are used in sculpture. Formed by the foaming reaction when two chemicals are mixed, they make an extremely lightweight material offering properties that make them excellent for insulation, protective packaging and similar industrial uses.

Expanded polystyrene is made from small bead-like granules which make it rather difficult to carve with a knife. This, unfortunately, is the more accessible of the two materials, being readily available from the packaging of many consumer items such as saucepans, electrical appliances, cameras, etc. It is also used for making ceiling and wall tiles.

Expanded polyurethane has many industrial uses but domestically it is most often seen coloured green and sold as the central support for flower arrangements. Its natural colour is usually white, grey or cream. Expanded polyurethane has a foam-like texture (it looks rather like a sponge) and makes an excellent medium to carve. It can be cut very easily with a bread saw, hacksaw blade or heated wire. Polyurethane is light to handle and can be rapidly carved. Holes can be cut through it and pieces glued together, although care must be taken to select a glue that does not react with the polyurethane. The relative cheapness of the material and its availability in large blocks makes it an ideal medium both for large scale sculpture and for working out ideas quickly in small sketch models.

Expanded polystyrene and polyurethane have the same disadvantages. Carving these materials makes a dust that clings to clothes, and the extreme lightness of this dust makes it rather difficult to sweep up. Inhaling it is a health hazard, which makes it advisable to cover the mouth and nose with a scarf. The lack of weight of these materials make them rather unsuitable for sculpture. This problem can be remedied and sculpture can be made stable by inserting a lump of lead or similarly heavy material into the base of the work. The appearance of expanded polystyrene and polyurethane is not very pleasing but the surface can be masked with a coat of resin, paint, plaster, papier maché or wax.

Obtaining expanded polystyrene and polyurethane

When ordering, be sure that it is *expanded* polystyrene or polyurethane that you ask for. Otherwise you are likely to be sent cans of the material in liquid form to expand for yourself! This is a more complicated procedure. Local firms selling either material can be found in the Yellow Pages of the telephone directory under 'Plastics' or 'Packaging Materials'.

Tools and equipment
　　Bench or table
　　Bread saw or hacksaw blade
　　Small serrated knife
　　Candle and matches (for heating knife)
　　Electric cutting tools (not essential)
　　Files, needle files, nail files, etc
　　Glasspaper

Block of expanded polystyrene (L) and polyurethane (R)

Tools for carving – serrated knife, breadsaw,
hacksaw blade, files, glasspaper and an electric
polystyrene cutter

Technique

The working method is the same for both
expanded polystyrene and expanded
polyurethane. Both come in the form of a large
block of the size and dimensions ordered.
Smaller blocks, of suitable size for carving, can
be cut from the main block with an ordinary
carpentry saw, or bread saw. Carving the
sculpture can be done with a small serrated
knife or hacksaw blade. Knives can be heated
slightly over a candle flame to make cutting
easier. Always keep the candle well away from
the expanded polystyrene or polyurethane as
both materials are highly flammable. There are

electrical tools on the market that are designed
specifically for cutting these materials. One
type is rather like a soldering iron, the other is
basically an electrically heated wire. These
tools make the rather awkward job of cutting
polystyrene considerably easier. Most
educational suppliers and the larger art shops
sell them.

Cutting and smoothing the surface can be
done with any fine file. Where small files are
unavailable a useful file for working recessed
surfaces and holes can be made by gluing
glasspaper onto a lolly stick. It is necessary to
use a strong rubberized glue such as *Evo-Stik*.

Blocks of expanded polystyrene or
polyurethane can be glued together with a PVA
glue or any of the brands sold in ironmongers
for sticking polystyrene tiles.

Cutting off a block from a length of expanded polyurethane

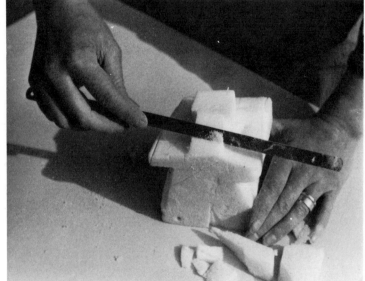

Carving a block of polyurethane with a hacksaw blade

After filing and glasspapering the surface the sculpture can be painted with a black wax to cover the 'foamed' texture of the expanded polyurethane

56

Children at Meadowlands County Junior
School carving small sculpture in expanded
polyurethane

Finishes

The surface of expanded polystyrene and
polyurethane is not very satisfactory for a
finished sculpture. The sponge-like surface is
rather unpleasant both in appearance and to
touch. It is also easily damaged. Generally,
some further treatment must be applied if the
sculpture is to be preserved.

Paint is a way of colouring the surface,
although it does not alter the texture very
much. As some types of gloss paint melt
polyurethane and polystyrene, it is important
to consult the paint dealer before buying the
paint. Emulsion paints are quite safe.

Plaster can be mixed and spread over the
surface with a knife, rather like spreading
butter. When the surface is covered and the
plaster has hardened it can be filed and
glasspapered to a smooth finish. This treatment
effectively covers the surface but is rather

brittle. Papier maché is a covering that will effectively disguise the porous look of the expanded polyurethane and polystyrene. For small sculptures and sketch models melted wax can be spread over the surface. This can be applied with a knife or brush. Melted candle wax can be used or paraffin wax can be ordered from a wax supplier. (See page 138.) This combination of materials is ideal where small work is to be sent to a bronze foundry for reproducing in bronze.

Seated Figures I and II
Sculpture cast into bronze. Sculpture made in expanded polyurethane can be cast into bronze a little cheaper. This is because the polyurethane can be burnt out of the plaster mould, which cuts out one of the processes. It is still of course very expensive.

Polyester resin makes a strong protective surface, though the use of resins is not recommended for the beginner. Packs of resin already pigmented with bronze, lead or other metals are a good method. The packs are supplied with comprehensive instructions for mixing the resin and hardener. The mixture can be spread over the surface of the polyurethane or polystyrene sculpture, giving a durable metal-like finish. The product is called *Devcon*. (See page 116 for details)
In the USA a similar product, but one which does not require mixing with a hardener, is metal modelling compound. This is a metal in paste form which can be applied as it is or thinned with a reducer to a consistency where it can be brushed or sprayed onto the surface.

Sculpture in expanded polyurethane by 9-year-olds from Meadowlands County Junior School. The giraffe was given a coat of gloss paint and the spots made by spraying paint from an aerosol can through a hole cut in a sheet of paper. The head, snail, and rat were painted with *Devcon* resin

New materials

There are many new materials that have appeared on the market in recent years. Most of these materials are marketed by educational equipment suppliers and have been developed for use in schools.

One of the most useful materials is self-hardening clay. This is ideal in situations where there is no access to a kiln for firing work. Self-hardening clay, of which there are many different brands available, can be treated in exactly the same way as ordinary clay (see page 37) but without the firing stage. To harden the clay some brands require painting with a coat of hardener that is sold with the clay, while others harden by being left to dry out completely.

Some of the more recent art materials available for sculpture. The photograph shows *Alostone*, a self-hardening clay with a sandy texture that can be modelled and carved. The round block is called *Formablock* which is a sand-coloured block that carves easily with knives, spoons and files. *Das* is a self-hardening clay that is widely available from art, craft and toy shops. The polythene bag contains a wood powder called *Instant Wood*, which can be mixed with water and formed into a block that can be carved when dry. The packet of hardener is for use on self-hardening clays. *Barbola Paste* can be formed into small blocks which can be carved when set. This is useful for detailed work. All these materials, except for the *Barbola Paste* and *Das* are available from the educational equipment suppliers given at the end of the book. *Barbola Paste* and *Das* can be bought from art shops. For materials available in the USA see page 140.

'Cat' carved from *Newclay* by a five year old child. (The makers of this product also sell glazes for painting over the *Newclay*)

Jewellery made from *Das*. The fruit and round bead necklace were rolled and sandpapered to shape. The daisies were cut from a piece of rolled out *Das* clay using a plain wedding ring (in the same way as a pastry cutter). Small V cuts were made in the discs of clay with a sharp knife to make the petal shapes and a pen top was pressed into the centre of each flower to make a slight indentation. When making beads to be threaded together it is important to make the holes before the clay has hardened. This can be done by pulling a needle threaded with a short piece of darning wool through each bead. The beads were all left to dry out before glasspapering, painting and varnishing with a coat of *Das* varnish.

Three figures carved from a lump of *Formablock*. Formablock looks rather like a hard block of sand. It is an excellent medium for even the youngest of children as it can be carved easily with very simple tools – junior saws, old hacksaw blades, knives, spoons or files. Although it is so soft to file and carve it has the substantial feel of a mineral, unlike many of the man-made plastic substances, such as expanded polyurethane

Figure in *Alostone*. This figure was roughly
shaped and then left to harden slightly before
being carved with a knife. *Alostone* is a self-
hardening clay but it has a sandy consistency
which gives the clay body and makes it pleasant
to work with. The sandy quality of the clay
gives the work a slightly rough, textured
appearance

Stone

Stone is one of the traditional materials of sculpture. Examples exist from pre-historic times, some having survived fire and the erosion of the elements in a way that no other sculpture material can. In our mechanised times carving stone with methods that have hardly altered for centuries gives the sculptor an added pleasure and link with the past.

Some people are deterred from stone carving because they think it must be an arduous and difficult way of making sculpture. For most people, however, it is a rewarding and satisfying medium which after all the stages of carving, filing and glasspapering, leaves one with a strong sense of achievement. The technique of carving stone is not difficult to learn and no special skills are required. Experience quickly teaches the beginner how hard to hit the chisel and which angles to avoid. Soon a rhythm will develop in the hammering that will become automatic and allow him to concentrate on the evolving shape of the stone. People who have had no success with clay or plasticine modelling are often surprised to find that they have a knowledge of shape and form that is better expressed in carving. Stone does not necessarily need to be carved in great detail and responds well to carving in strong bold forms. It can be carved by most age groups. Even primary age children will find stone carving well within their scope, although they might need to choose a soft stone which can be carved with knives and files rather than with hammer and chisels.

Types of stone

All stone falls geologically into one of three groups:

Igneous – formed by the action of fire, eg granite

Sedimentary – caused by the action of water, eg limestone

Metamorphic – rocks, mostly of the igneous or sedimentary type, that have been further altered as a result of pressure accompanied by heat, eg marble, which is geologically a limestone that has been recrystalized.

Sandstones Sandstones are porous but compact and durable. They consist of fine grains of sand cemented together. There is great variation in the hardness of sandstones depending on the porosity of the material and whether the cementing material is hard or soft. Sandstones quarried in Devonshire and Cheshire are excellent for sculpture purposes.

The Venus of Willendorf, Upper Palaeolithic, Vienna, one of the earliest known carvings

A collection of different types of stone suitable for carving. There is a vast range of different types and colours of stone suitable for carving. Some of the best known of these include sandstone and limestones, marble, soapstone, steatite and alabaster

Limestone Composed mainly of calcium carbonate, limestone is formed by the skeletal remains of shellfish and minute organisms. Limestone has a sandy granular texture and varies in hardness and compactness. It has been used as a carving medium from antiquity. Limestone varies from natural chalk to very hard stones that are crystalline, rather like marble. This type is capable of taking a polish. There is a wide range of colours – grey, buff, cream, yellow, blue, red, green and brown. Many counties in England quarry limestone suitable for carving: Clipsham stone quarried in the County of Leicestershire, Hornton stone quarried in the county of Oxfordshire,

Portland stone from Portland, Dorset. There are also plentiful supplies in America and France.

Soapstone A grainy black, grey or green stone that is very soft to carve but which polishes to a rich, glossy shine. This stone is ideal for beginners and experienced sculptors alike. It is the stone used so often by the Eskimos for their carvings.

Alabaster Alabaster is a form of gypsum. This is another soft stone that can be polished to a rich shine. Alabaster knives are made for carving the stone, as it is so soft. It can also be carved with wood or stone carving chisels. It is an encouraging type of stone for beginners to work with, although like soapstone it is also

Two Figures. Alabaster. Glynis Beecroft

popular with professional sculptors. Alabaster is available in many colours from white to grey and pink tints. When buying a block it is important to check that it is sound. Sometimes there are layers of a soft mud-like substance that make areas of it difficult to carve. Wetting the block should reveal these flaws. Finished sculpture in alabaster must be handled carefully as its softness means that it scratches easily. Alabaster is suitable only for indoor sculpture.

Marble This is a beautiful stone when finished and has been used by the most famous sculptors from Michelangelo to Henry Moore. Marble is a hard stone to carve and should be reserved for the time when the sculptor has become experienced and competent in carving. Marble is available in a vast range of colours and varies in the degree of hardness. When carving, it is advisable to use a marble claw, which has much finer teeth.

Two other types of stone that have not been mentioned are *granite* and *slate*. Both have a wide range of colours and polish to a high shine. Granite is extremely hard and not suitable for beginners. Slate varies in its hardness but requires careful carving as it has a tendency to split off in layers.

Obtaining stone

Quarries Many counties quarry stone which is suitable for carving. A visit to the local quarry for advice is the best way to find out whether the stone is suitable for sculpture purposes. Buying from quarries is usually the cheapest way of obtaining stone. Often pieces are almost given away.

A useful booklet is available, giving all the information concerning quarries in the counties of Britain, with addresses, type and colour of stone and other details. The description to look for is 'monumental' which means that the stone is suitable for carving. The book is called *The Natural Stone Directory* and is published by: Stone Industries, Park Lane Publications Ltd, 70 Chiswick High Street, London W4.

Aurora. Slate. Margaret Lovell

Demolished buildings Stone can often be acquired when old buildings such as churches and hospitals are being demolished. It is best to contact the site foreman or contractor, who may be only too pleased to have some one take it away. A good idea if you can not identify the stone is to take a hammer and chisel with you. A quick chip at the stone will enable you to decide whether it is soft enough to carve.

Stone masons Stone masons will sometimes sell off odd pieces of stone at a reasonable price. Addresses can be found in the Yellow Pages of the telephone directory under such headings as 'Stone Masons', 'Stone Merchants', and 'Monumental Masons'.

Sturdy table suitable for stone carving

Stone suppliers Many schools and colleges order from a firm that supplies stone and tools. Marble, chalk, soapstone, alabaster, limestone, etc can all be ordered by the sackful. The main drawback is the cost of the carriage, which in some cases exceeds that of the material itself. Blocks of a specific size can be sawn to order.

Storing stone
Although some of the harder types of stone can be kept outside, most stones for sculpture are best protected. A corner of the sculpture room or studio or an old shed should be set aside as a storage place. If this is not possible, a sheet of polythene wrapped around the stone is some protection from the frost.

Testing stone
Before buying stone it can be tested for soundness by tapping it with a metal hammer. If there is a clear ringing noise it should be a sound piece of stone. Wetting it reveals any obvious faults.

Tools and equipment
Stone carving is not an expensive craft to start. For a fairly reasonable expenditure a simple set of carving tools can be bought, which will be quite adequate for learning to carve in stone. In addition to this a stout table or bench is essential, and a place to work such as a shed or room where stone dust and chippings can be tolerated.

It is surprising that stone carving tools have altered so little through the ages. In Greek times they were using points, toothed and flat chisels, rasps, files and abrasives, just as we do today. The only additions that we have made to the stone carver's equipment are electric sanders, saws and pneumatic hammers, which are specialized tools. Nothing really is quite as versatile for carving as the traditional hammer and chisel.

The beginner should be able to manage with a small number of tools that can be added to when he feels confident of his interest in carving. A basic set of stone carving tools should consist of three chisels with different ends designed for the three stages of carving. These three chisels are known as the point, claw and flat chisel. In addition a hammer

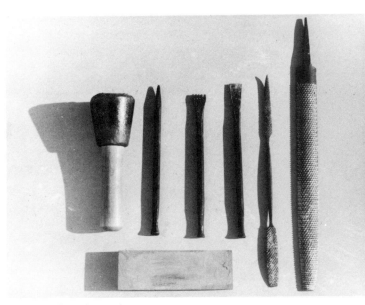

Basic set of carving tools

called the dummy mallet is needed for hitting the chisels, a rasp for smoothing surfaces and a riffler for filing parts that are difficult to reach. A sharpening stone is required for sharpening chisels

Point   The point is used for the preliminary rough shaping of the sculpture. It removes pieces of stone quickly, leaving grooves in the surface of the sculpture. When carving soft stone this stage is often left out and the claw is the first chisel used. Points are sold in three sizes: light, medium and heavy. The most useful to start with is the medium point.

Points should be held firmly. Hard blows to the point with the hammer will remove lumps cleanly. Points should be held at an angle of 45° to the surface of the sculpture, which will allow pieces of stone to break away from the main block. It is important not to allow the point to become too deeply wedged or it will shear off.

Carving with a point chisel held at an angle of 45°

Claw This is used for the second stage of carving. It will remove the deep grooves made by the point so that the sculpture may be more precisely defined. The claw leaves the sculpture covered with fine lines. Claws are sold in a variety of widths. A useful size to start with is 9 mm ($\frac{3}{8}$ in). The claw is similar to the flat chisel except for the cutting edge which consists of a straight row of flat or pointed teeth.

Virgin and Child with St John (Taddei Madonna) 1504–6 by Michelangelo. Note the many lines made with the claw chisel

Flat chisel   The flat chisel is used for the final stage of carving. It leaves the sculpture with a fairly smooth surface. The most useful size to buy at first is the 9 mm width. Flat chisels are used as a surface finishing tool when the shaping of the stone with the claw chisel has been completed. Flat chisels are not used very much by some sculptors who prefer to go from the claw chisel to abrasives. The best known example of this technique can be found in the sculpture of Michelangelo. However, this missing out of the stage of carving with the flat chisel is not recommended for inexperienced sculptors. Work with the flat chisel can be an important stage in the final defining of forms. By removing the lines made by the claw, the flat areas can reveal imperfections in the carving that need alteration before the final stage with abrasives.

Dummy mallet   The dummy mallet is used for both stone and wood carving. It is more suitable for the softer stones and is generally used for mallet headed chisels. It makes a compact weight to handle and is the best choice for a beginner.

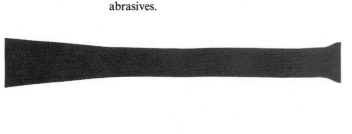

Chisels are made with two different shaped hammering ends. These are called hammer head chisels and mallet head chisels. Hammer head chisels are for use on hard stones while mallet head chisels are used on soft stones. Mallet head chisels can also be used with wood mallets as the dome-shaped end will not damage them. The most useful type to start with are the mallet head chisels.

Hammer head

Mallet head

Stone rasp   The stone rasp is used for the initial rough filing of the sculpture. For a smoother finish either an ordinary file or a coarse sheet of glasspaper can be used.

Riffler   This double-ended file is used for reaching awkward places that cannot be reached with straight files. There are a number of different shaped ends to choose from. The most useful shapes are the ones that incorporate a curved and a tapered end.

A more comprehensive set of stone carving tools. This shows the lump hammer, dummy mallet, point, claw, and flat chisels, the bullnose, gouge and pitcher chisels, the bouchard hammer, sharpening stone, riffler, file and rasp

Adding more tools to the basic set
In addition to buying smaller and larger points, claws and flat chisels, there are three other types of chisel that should be mentioned. These are the pitcher, gouge and bullnose chisel.

Pitcher   A wide chisel used for knocking off corners and edges of a block to give the sculpture its rough shape before carving.

Gouge   For carving into concave shapes.

Bullnose   Similar to a flat chisel but with rounded edges. Used for carving into shapes where the corners of a normal chisel would dig into the sculpture.

Bouchard hammer   The bouchard or bush hammer is essentially a multi-point or multi-pick. It looks rather like a metal-headed steak hammer. Used directly on the stone, its function is to wear down the surface in broad uniform layers by a process of pulverization. The pitted texture that it leaves can be removed with a flat chisel or file. It is useful when carving the less compact types of stone that have a tendency to splinter off with a hammer or chisel. It is also useful for modelling curved shapes or for adding a texture to the stone.

Lump hammer   The lump hammer is for use with hammer headed tools and is generally used for carving the harder stones.

Sharpening chisels

Tools blunt quite rapidly on hard stones and will need fairly frequent sharpening. This can be done on a flat piece of York paving stone, or a coarse sharpening stone. The method is to stroke the chisel along the length of the sharpening stone using water as a lubricant. The chisel should be pushed away from the body in contact with the stone and lifted back for the next stroke.

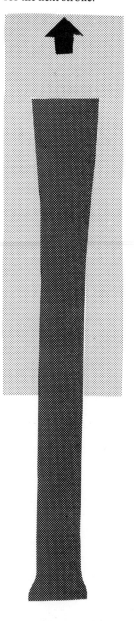

Abrasives

There are two basic types of abrasive tool:
1 metal rasps and files
2 stone and mineral abrasives

Rasps and files   The difference between rasps and files is in the abrasive surface. *Rasps* are made up of small projections in the metal. They vary in coarseness and are suitable for rasping rough surfaces to make them fairly smooth. Their metal projections cut into the stone quickly and evenly. Rasps tend to leave lines in the stone.

Files are made with lines cut into the metal surface. They are also made in varying degrees of coarseness. The finer the file the smoother the finish that may be achieved. A very fine file needs frequent cleaning with a wire brush to prevent clogging with stone dust.

Stone and mineral abrasives   are useful for the final stage of smoothing and polishing the sculpture. Usually they are applied after the sculpture has been filed. The stone is rubbed over the surface working an area at a time. Pieces of stone for smoothing stone surfaces can be bought from ironmongers and sculpture suppliers. There is a variety of types of abrasive including carborundum, emery and pumice. Pieces of sandstone can be used for smoothing the softer stones. Fine emery cloth, glasspaper and carborundum paper are also used for finishing sculpture. Soft abrasive powders can be used for polishing stones.

Care of tools

Tools should be kept clean and sharp. If tools are kept in a damp atmosphere such as a garden shed, it is advisable to oil them lightly to help prevent them from rusting.

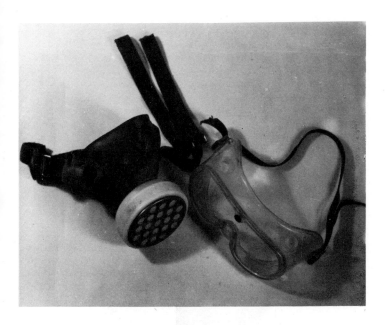

Protective goggles and mask

It is advisable to use goggles or protective glasses while carving stone. They are particularly important during the roughing out stage, when chips are flying with some force. It is essential that masks or respirators are worn when using sanding attachments on an electric drill. If respirators are not worn when carving silicates (for example some of the sandstones) silicosis could develop.

Protective goggles and respirator

Electric drill and attachments for buffing, polishing and abrading

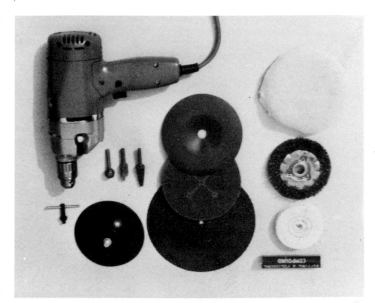

Sanding discs

There is a wide variety of sanding discs. These are fixed to a rubber backing pad and fitted to an electric drill. This makes the final abrading stage considerably quicker. Sanding with an electric drill should really be done out of doors.

Disadvantages of using sanding discs are that the cooling fan on the electric drill blows the stone dust over a considerable area; the face, hair and clothes need to be protected; and there is a tendency to remove the stone in planes so that qualities achieved with chisels and files are lost.

Only the broadest parts of the sculpture can be reached, although small abrasive attachments can be bought for reaching the more inaccessible parts.

Technique
Carving a lump of soapstone

Before doing any carving, examine the lump of
stone from all angles to decide what shape you
can see in it. If you already have an idea in
mind, study the stone to see how the idea is best
fitted into the stone. Making drawings in
charcoal on paper often helps to clarify one's
ideas

Just to show how the unexpected has to be incorporated into a new idea. The stone was drawn on with charcoal, in preparation for a carving based on a 'mother and child' theme. After some preliminary roughing out with a chisel, a fault in the stone became evident and a large piece of stone fell away

Block turned on its side, which suggested some sort of animal shape

Charcoal lines drawn directly on block to
clarify shape for carving

Because soapstone is soft and fractures easily
the rough carving is done with a claw chisel
instead of the point chisel

Detail of carving with the claw chisel

Detail of working with flat chisel. The flat chisel removes the grooves made in the stone by the claw chisel

Some areas of the stone were not compact
enough to carve with a chisel. To prevent
lumps 'pecking' out these surfaces were shaped
with the bouchard hammer

Detail of bouchard hammer hitting the stone
surface directly to wear it away by
pulverization

Smoothing the sculpture with a stone rasp

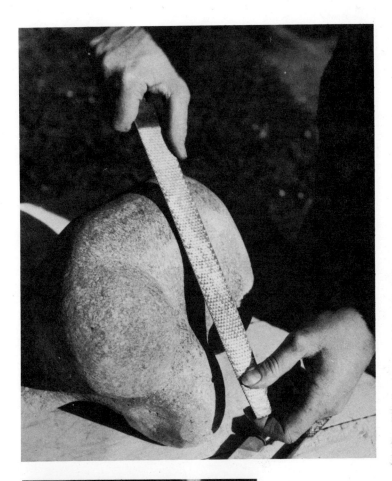

The broadest areas of the sculpture were
smoothed using a sanding disc attachment on
an electric drill

Finish

A very fine finish can be achieved by using several grades of silicon carbide paper (usually called 'wet and dry' paper). Start with the coarsest, rubbing a small area at a time with a circular motion until the whole surface has been done. Always keep enough water between the abrasive paper and the sculpture to make a creamy paste. This will prevent scratching. Proceed with all the grades from the coarsest to the finest. When too much paste builds up wash it away with a wet cloth, and at the same time check that there are no patches that are missed. Wet and dry paper lasts longer if the water is flicked directly onto the stone rather than immersing the wet and dry in the bowl of water. Repeated soaking causes wet and dry paper to disintegrate very quickly

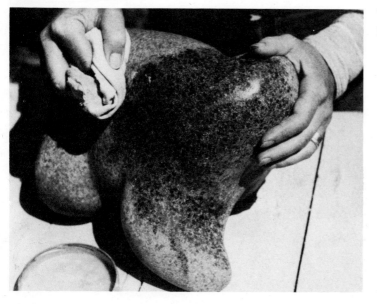

When the sculpture is smooth it can be polished with beeswax

Buffing the waxed sculpture with a polishing mop attachment on an electric drill. The lambswool bonnet in the front of the picture is an attachment that can be used on the drill to add a high gloss to the sculpture surface. (It is not necessary to use an electric drill and polishing attachments – all the polishing can be done by hand with a duster)

Detail of polished surface

Completed sculpture

NOTE   Not all types of stone will take a polish. With most of the sandstones and limestones the final polishing stage is omitted. The last stage is abrading with carborundum paper or glasspaper. It is not necessary to use water as a lubricant.

Preparing Beeswax

Beeswax can be bought in the form of a hard block from chemists, upholsterers and sculpture suppliers. Before it can be used it must be melted into a small quantity of warm turpentine to soften it (roughly equal proportions of each). The turpentine should be *gently* heated in a double burner saucepan. Remember that the turpentine is highly flammable and you should not take your eyes off it for a moment while it is being heated. When warm add the beeswax, stir gently until dissolved and leave to cool.

Baby. Alabaster by Patrick Baker, aged 7 years

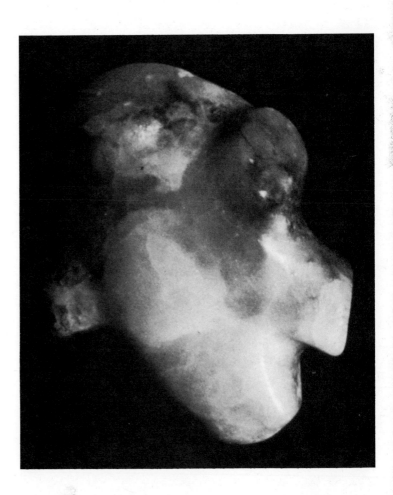

Wood

Wood is one of the traditional materials for carving. It is one of the oldest forms of sculpture, and has been used as a carving medium for over 5,000 years. The warmth and mellowness of carving a material that has spent most of its life as a living growing thing adds a unique quality that is special to wood.

Wood is abundant in most parts of the world. Every piece of wood is different; there is an infinite variety of colour, shape and degree of hardness and softness.

Types of wood
Wood falls into two types, both of which are suitable for carving. These are:
Hardwood – not necessarily a 'hard' wood – from trees with broad, flat leaves of the deciduous variety, eg oak and chestnut.
Softwood – which may not be a 'soft' wood – from trees with narrow resinous leaves. These are of the coniferous variety and include the pine and hemlock. Yew is an example of a 'hard' softwood.

The ease with which wood can be carved with hand tools varies considerably. It is helpful to know which woods are easy to carve and which hard to carve. A short list of the better known woods is given below.

SOFTWOODS

Easy to work	*Fairly difficult to work*
Cedar of Lebanon	Fir
Pine	Hemlock
	Redwood
	Spruce
	Difficult to work
	Douglas fir
	Larch
	Yew

HARDWOODS

Easy to work	*Difficult to work*
Willow	Ash
Yellow poplar	Beech
Limewood	Birch
Mahogany	Cherry
	Walnut
	Ebony
	Elm
	Mahogany (varies)
	Oak
	Rosewood

Blocks of wood suitable for carving

Obtaining wood

The most expensive woods to buy are generally those from wood importers. Where good quality or rare types of wood are required this is the place from which to buy. There are a number of wood importers.

Wood yards and timber merchants deal in long lengths of wood supplied to the building industry. Offcuts can be purchased cheaply from joiners and cabinet makers. Generally, domestic woods are the most economical to buy, imported woods the most expensive. When buying a block for carving in the round make sure that it is thick enough for carving. A piece 9×9 cm ($3\frac{1}{2} \times 3\frac{1}{2}$ in.) is a good thickness to ask for. Planks about 25 mm (1 in.) thick are useful for relief carving. Addresses of local firms can be found in the Yellow Pages of the telephone directory under the headings – 'Timber Importers' and 'Timber Merchants'.

There is plenty of wood around that costs nothing more than the time taken to find it. Places to look are in woods, hedgerows and the sea shore. Fallen branches can provide interesting ready-made shapes for carving. Driftwood is often well seasoned and only requires storing under cover to dry it out.

Old unwanted pieces of furniture provide interesting wood to carve. Where old telegraph poles or railway sleepers are available, they can be sawn up to make good sized blocks. Cut logs are another readily available supply of wood in country areas. Even in towns, logs are often sawn up when trees are felled. Here, the local authority parks department is the best source to contact. Logs from recently felled trees need to be well seasoned, a process taking several years. It is a good policy for the serious woodcarver to keep a supply of wood seasoning in the corner of the studio.

A weathered piece of wood of the type that can be found in woods and hedgerows

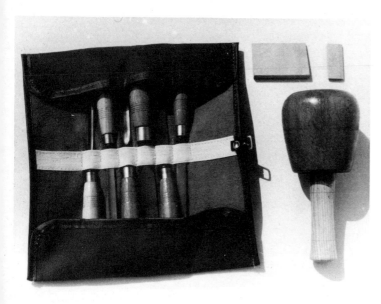

A basic set of woodcarving chisels, including canvas case, wood mallet and sharpening stones

Tools and equipment
Strong bench or table
Vice or G cramp
Set of wood carving chisels
Wood mallet
Rasps and files
Glasspaper
Sharpening stone
Working in wood means investing in a good set of wood chisels. Although the initial cost might seem rather high, the tools, with care, will last a lifetime.

Chisels There are hundreds of different shapes and sizes to choose from. The best policy for the student woodcarver is to buy a relatively small working kit, consisting of a few basic chisels and a mallet. These can be added to later. It is important not to economise on quality. Chisel handles must be of good quality wood to withstand the force of mallet blows. Ash handles are a reliable type to choose. Some beginners like to buy a set of chisels in a canvas case. Professional woodcarvers sometimes deliberately buy chisels with different handles to help identify them quickly when working.

A more comprehensive set of woodcarving chisels and sharpening stones

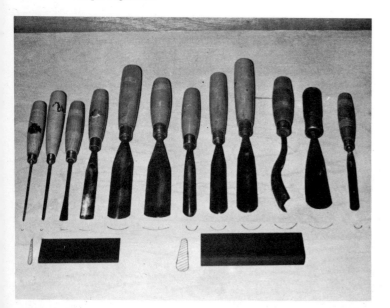

Chisels have straight cutting edges and are
available in many sizes. The sharp edge cuts
into the wood, while the thickness of the chisel
(bevel) serves as a wedge to force the wood
apart

Gouges are tools with curved cutting edges.
There are many varieties of gouge. The type
with a bent shank is used for deep cutting

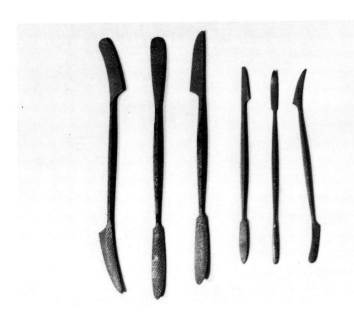

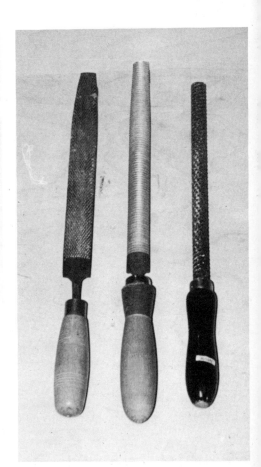

Rifflers (double-ended files) are useful for
reaching awkward parts of the sculpture

A selection of rasps and surforms are useful for
filing the wood

Care of tools

Woodcarving tools need frequent honing, as their edge must be razor sharp for best results. Both chisels and gouges are honed by rubbing against an abrasive surface. An ordinary fine-textured oilstone is used for this purpose. A few drops of light machine oil are used to lubricate the oilstone surface, so that excessive friction and heat is avoided. Woodcarving tools are honed on both sides, unlike joiners' tools, which are honed only on the bevelled edge. Chisels are easier to hone than gouges. A small amount of oil is dropped on the oilstone and the chisel is placed so that the bevel is flat on the stone. The chisel is moved forwards and backwards along the length of the stone. To test for sharpness, hold the edge of the chisel up to the light. The chisel is sharp if no line of light is visible along its cutting edge. At this stage, the other side of the chisel is honed to approximately the same angle. The total angle between the honed edges should be about 30°.

To hone a gouge, put a few drops of lubricating oil on the oilstone, and hold the gouge at right angles with it, making sure that the bevelled surface lies flat on the stone. Now move the gouge sideways along the length of the stone and back again repeatedly. At the same time rock the gouge from side to side, so that every part of the bevel comes in contact with the stone. Honing the other side of a gouge is done with a slipstone. Slipstones are made in the same abrasive stone as the oilstone but are wedge-shaped with two rounded edges to suit gouges of varying curve. After applying oil the slip is rubbed backwards and forwards on the inside of the gouge. It is held so that the inner bevel is formed at an angle which is about the same as that of the outer bevel. Honing produces a burr along the cutting edge of the tool. This is removed by stroking the edge with a specially prepared piece of leather, called a strop. When the cutting edge of a wood carving tool becomes dull, it can be restored by stropping, though further honing will eventually have to be done.

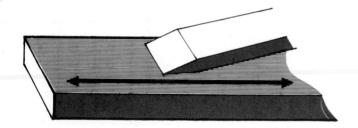

Sharpening a chisel

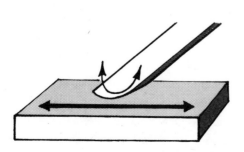

Sharpening a gouge

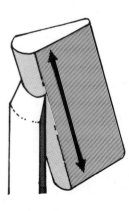

Vices, cramps, etc

Large blocks of wood are held in place by their own physical weight and no vice is required. Small blocks need to be held securely by means of a bench or table vice. They are occasionally held in the hand, but this is not recommended, as it is too easy for a chisel to slip, causing a nasty cut. If the wood is held in a metal bench or table vice, the inner clasping surfaces should be lined with broad strips of thick leather or felt to prevent damage to the sculpture. If wooden clamps are used, this is unnecessary. Where neither type of vice is available G-cramps can be purchased from any good ironmonger. By cramping the wood to the bench the work is held steady. (See page 19)

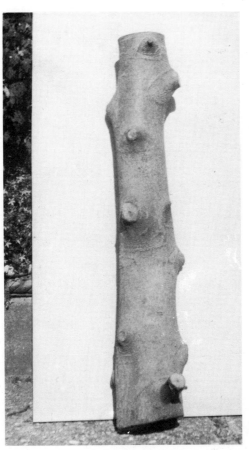

Technique

Wood carving is a difficult branch of sculpture, requiring experience and knowledge of wood. Although some sculptors prefer working with hardwoods, the student woodcarver is recommended to start with a soft wood such as lime, soft pine or a soft variety of mahogany. When he has gained knowledge and experience of working in wood and a thorough knowledge of his tools, he will feel ready to work some of the harder woods. It is worth remembering that rounded, compact forms are the most suitable to start with.

Projections such as arms and legs will lead to problems. Teachers of woodcarving often start their students off with a very simple form to carve. A leaf shape or a relief carving using a flat piece of wood is often chosen for a first carving. Carving a flat surface on one side only is a good introduction to carving. Carving a small sculpture in the round is reserved for the time when the student has familiarized himself with his woodcarving tools.

Before starting work on the piece of wood, it should be carefully and thoroughly studied. Much time and effort can be saved by cutting away unwanted masses with a saw. It is helpful while making decisions about shape and form to draw on the wood with chalk or charcoal. Unwanted areas can be cross-hatched to indicate that they are to be removed.

The gouge is generally used for blocking out initial masses and for carving hardwoods. Fairly large, broad tools are the most suitable for the preliminary roughing out stages. As the work progresses flat chisels and finer gouges are used and a lighter mallet can replace the heavy one used for the rough work. It is important to follow the grain of the wood. Finally, the work can be smoothed with Surforms, wood rasps and files. The surface can then be finished with glasspaper.

Stages of carving

Original log of wood from which the carving is to be made

Removing the bark with a draw knife. This two handled blade can be kept very sharp and is useful for stripping off the bark quickly. It is not essential and a wide chisel can be used instead

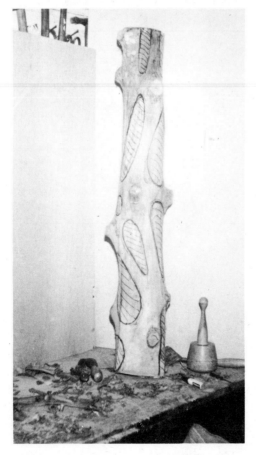

After stripping off the bark the design is drawn on and the areas to be removed are indicated. The sculptor's intention is to produce an outer form enclosing an inner one. The oval shapes that have lines drawn on them will be cut away to become 'windows' through which the inner form can be seen

Carving the oval shapes of the sculpture. The cuts are made from the outside edge into the centre with a wide gouge to make a dish shape

The sculptor drills through from one dish shape to another making a tunnel over which the outer surface forms a bridge. The drill holes can be enlarged using a gouge

Cleaning up the surface with a rasp

Glasspapering the surface gives the sculpture a very smooth finish. Glasspaper should be wrapped round a piece of wood or cork to make a firm rubbing surface. A coarse grade of glasspaper should be used, progressing to a medium and then a fine grade

The completed sculpture. *Form in Tension.*
Oak. Clive Nethercott. The wood was sealed by
brushing on a coat of French polish. When the
polish was dry it was rubbed down with flour
paper (a very fine abrasive paper) to remove
the shine and leave a more natural finish. The
sculpture was mounted on a granite base

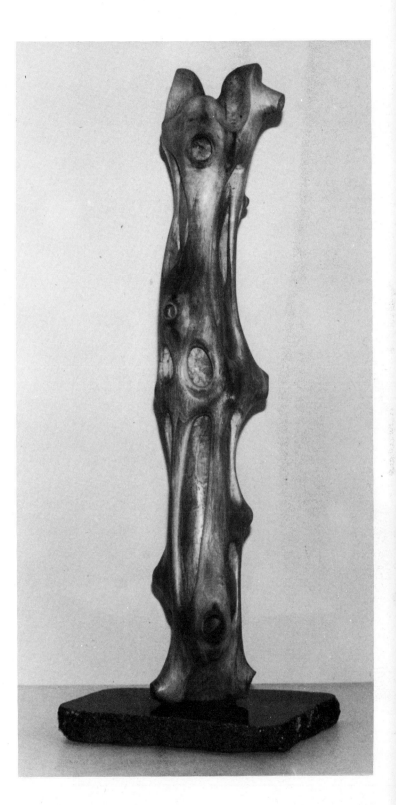

Finishes

The type of finish applied to the sculpture depends very much on the work itself. The sculpture surface can be left with chisel marks showing, or it can be made completely smooth. Wood can be painted, stained, waxed, oiled or

Ivy Embrace. Ivy and Beech wood. Ben Barker

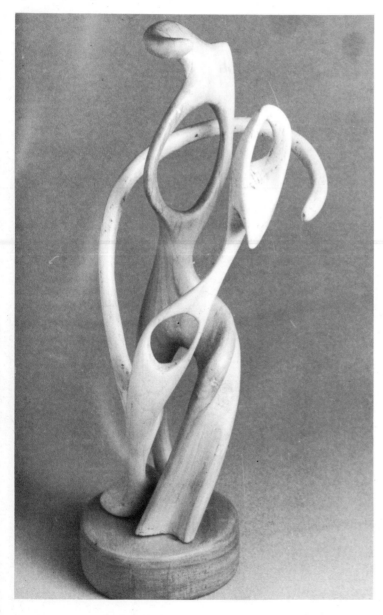

varnished. Masking the natural colour and texture of the wood is not recommended, as the grain in most wood carvings is an important feature of the sculpture. The usual method uses wax or oil to protect the wood while bringing out the rich quality of the grain.

Light oils such as teak oil are suitable for protecting wood sculpture. These will preserve and enhance the wood while retaining the natural matt finish. Light oils for wood are obtainable from hardware, ironmongers and do-it-yourself shops. A recipe for beeswax is given on page 83. Beeswax gives wood sculpture a glossier surface than oil.

A still higher shine can be achieved by using a varnish instead of oil or wax. This makes a durable surface that requires no further attention. (Oiled and waxed sculptures occasionally require a further application when kept in a dry atmosphere). There are many different varnishes on the market. Polyurethane varnish is one of the hardest and most durable of the modern varnishes. Shellac and button polish were the traditional ways of sealing wood. All types of wood varnish do to some extent mask the natural quality of the wood.

Staining is a way of altering the colour of the wood to a darker shade. Stain can be bought in a variety of wood colours, eg walnut, teak and mahogany. Colour charts are available in most shops that sell wood stain. The liquid that holds the coloured stain in suspension is known as the vehicle. There are a variety of vehicles, the choice of which determines the effect that it will have on the wood:

Water vehicles – raise the grain of the wood slightly

Oil vehicles – penetrate the surface superficially. They do not affect the wood grain. Polyurethane varnishes should not be used over this type of stain

Varnish vehicles – do not raise the wood grain. The mixture should be thoroughly stirred. It gives a high, richly coloured gloss that masks the original quality of the wood. Polyurethane can be bought with a stain added.

Seasoning

Well-seasoned wood is best for carving. The use of unseasoned wood (green wood) may result in irreparable damage as a result of shrinking and cracking. The best policy is to acquire wood, seal the cut ends with paint to prevent rapid drying out and set it aside in a bin or a corner of the studio. It must age for about 2 years in an even temperature with a good circulation of air around the blocks. A wise precaution is to paint or chalk the date on each block before storing it. This will prevent mistakes in remembering how long a block has been seasoning. Wood bought from reputable firms for the purpose of carving will have been seasoned.

Untitled sculpture. Elm wood. David Thomas

96

Madonna. Mahogany. Clive Nethercott

Recumbent Figure. Elm wood. Ben Barker

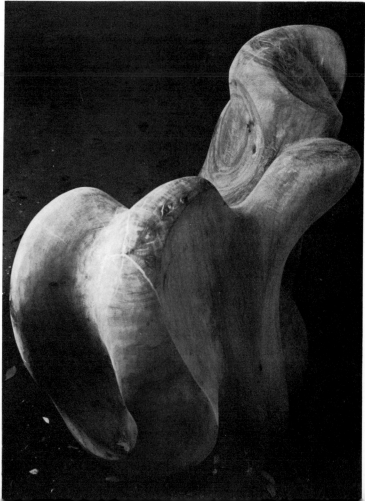

Reclining Figure. Elm wood. Henry Moore

A chalk quarry

Chalk

Chalk is a white or grey, loosely coherent type of limestone rock, composed almost entirely of the calcerous remains of minute marine organisms and fragments of shell.

Chalk is an ideal medium to choose for a first attempt at carving, and forms good experience before carving stone. While being soft and easy to carve, it also possesses many of the qualities of stone. Chalk can be found in many areas of Britain and is one of the cheapest materials for carving.

Random lumps of chalk

Obtaining chalk

Large quantities of chalk are quarried in England in the counties of Kent, Sussex, Hampshire, Cambridgeshire and Lincolnshire. Chalk can also be found in some of the surrounding counties, often lying in fields, on the face of hills or where excavations have been made. Where there is plenty of chalk lying around, pieces can be individually selected. Choosing a shape that suggests a particular idea provides a good starting point for a carving. It is a good idea to select several pieces so that they can be studied in more detail at home before a final selection is made. Remember that if the chalk has been recently gathered it is likely to be too wet to carve and will need a day or two to dry out.

Where chalk is unobtainable from natural sources, a local stone mason can sometimes advise on the nearest source. Chalk can also be bought from chalk quarries. If there are any locally, their addresses can be found in the Yellow Pages of the telephone directory listed under the heading 'Limeworks'. A sack of random lumps of chalk can be ordered from Shearman and Company Ltd, Vicarage Road, Abbotskerswell, Newton Abbot, Devon. The disadvantage of buying chalk in this way is that the carriage costs can be considerably more than the cost of the chalk.

Tools and equipment
Heavy table or bench
Folded piece of sacking on which to stand chalk
Hammer and stonecarving chisels
Rasps and files
Glasspaper

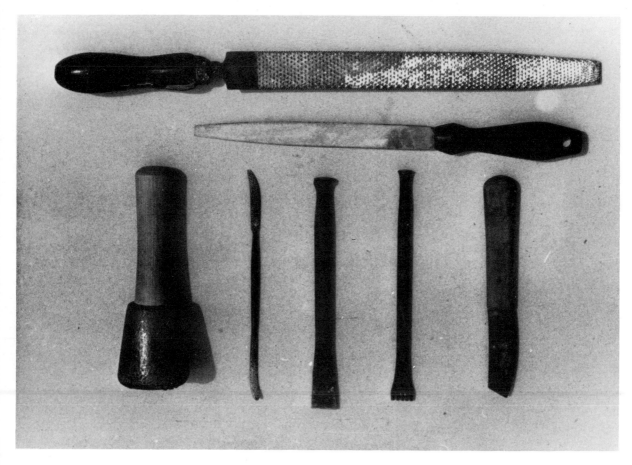

Tools for carving chalk

Technique

The procedure for carving chalk is very like that for carving stone. The tools and equipment are the same and so are the working methods.

Before attempting any carving, set aside some time to study the piece of chalk. Place it where it can be seen from all angles and carefully observe its shape and form. When familiar with the shape and its possibilities, make a few drawings. Charcoal is a good medium for sculpture drawings as it can be quickly altered and smudged as ideas are decided. When the final sculpture idea has been worked out it can be drawn directly onto the chalk with a piece of charcoal. Areas to be cut away can be cross-hatched.

Lump of chalk

Shape for sculpture drawn onto chalk. Areas to
be removed have been cross-hatched

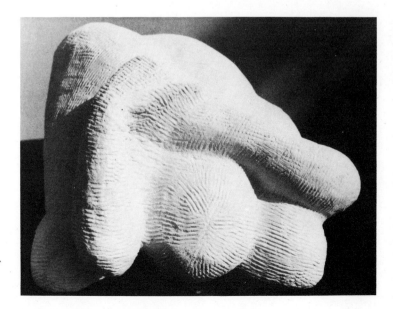

Sculpture given its shape by carving with a claw
chisel and hammer. The lines are made by the
pointed teeth of the claw chisel

Removing the claw marks with a flat chisel. As the chalk is quite soft it is not always necessary to use a hammer at this stage

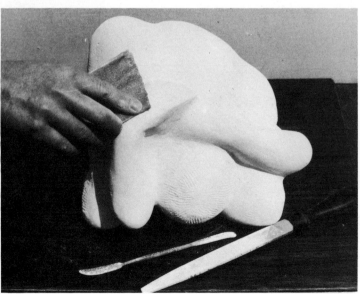

Glasspapering the surface of the sculpture will result in a very smooth finish

Finishes

Leaving the carved surface of a piece of chalk untreated is not really practical as chalk loses its whiteness through the dust and dirt in the atmosphere. It also sheds chalk dust when moved or handled. To prevent this it can be painted with a couple of coats of clear shellac or varnish. Alternatively, it can be painted with a washable white emulsion paint. Both treatments obliterate the appearance of the natural chalk. Chalk can be treated with any of the finishes that are applied to plaster, including gloss, emulsion and enamel paint, metallic finishes, stains and polyurethane varnishes. (See chapter on plaster finishes, page 115)

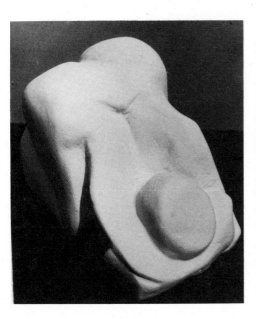

Kneeling Figure by Edwin Beecroft

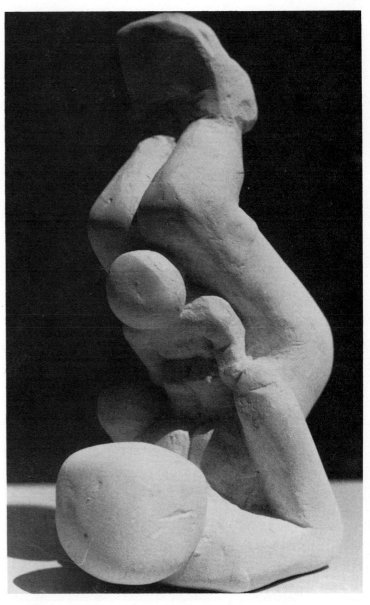

Mother and Child by Clare Alexander

Plaster

Plaster of paris derives its name from the earth around Paris and the surrounding regions, which contains an abundance of gypsum from which plaster of paris is manufactured. Gypsum is a mineral which was formed by the depositing of salts in inland lakes during the course of many geological periods. As these lakes dried and as the surface formation of the region was altered, the mineral formed was buried to varying depths.

The gypsum is quarried from underground deposits forming a solid crystalline mass. The plaster of paris is manufactured by heating the gypsum to a high temperature which partially calcinates or dehydrates it. When the roasted powder is mixed with sufficient water to form a mass of creamy consistency the chemical reaction causes it to thicken and set hard. It is this property of plaster of paris that makes it one of the most versatile and extensively used of all the sculpture materials.

Plaster has a wide range of uses. It can be modelled by adding and building up the sculpture, or it can be carved by chiselling away the block. Plaster is also used for making moulds and has a wide range of industrial applications in the field of casting. Many sculptors make their work in plaster before sending it away to be cast in a more durable material such as bronze.

Like most materials, plaster also has disadvantages. Although soft and easy to carve, it is best carved slightly damp. This means that the chippings stick together to form a sludge which makes it rather messy to work with. This is best tackled by developing a workman-like approach and cleaning up at frequent intervals. The other disadvantage is that although plaster sets hard it still requires careful handling as its chips easily.

Obtaining plaster

Plaster of paris is manufactured by British Gypsum Limited, who supply all grades of Industrial Plaster to builders merchants. There are merchants who specialize in the re-packing of these grades into smaller bags. In these smaller packs plaster can be bought from art suppliers, art shops, large ironmongers and some of the larger chemists. Boots Chemists stock plaster of paris (dental plaster) in large and small quantities. At branches where it is not stocked it may be ordered.

The grades most suitable for casting plaster blocks to carve are the casting plasters, of which Fine Casting plaster is the best. Dental plaster is a similar material but it has a shorter setting time. All the casting grades yield a plaster which is easy to carve.

Always store plaster in a dry place. If damp gets to the plaster it will lose its setting power. Large quantities can be stored in a plastic dustbin. Smaller quantities are best stored in an airtight tin or plastic container. (The large polythene containers that ice cream is sold in are ideal.) The serviceable life of plaster depends upon climatic and storage conditions. The material should be used (according to British Gypsum) within a period of three months from the date of manufacture. (In the author's own experience plaster often lasts many months longer than this and is still perfectly suitable for sculpture purposes.)

Tools and equipment

Plaster adheres strongly to materials of metal, wood etc but cracks away easily from polythene and other plastic materials. It is advisable to work on polythene or newspaper to protect the table or bench. Bowls for mixing plaster should all be of polythene. Where small amounts of plaster need to be mixed, children's footballs cut in half make good containers. By flexing them or turning them inside out hardened plaster falls away easily.

Stone carving chisels may be used for carving plaster. These can be of the pointed, toothed or flat type but they should be used with care as plaster is a more fragile material than stone. Alternatively, wood chisels (preferably old ones) can be used. Mallet blows should not be too hard and chisels should not be permitted to become wedged in the plaster. Chisels should be carefully cleaned after coming in contact with plaster. Any plaster stuck to them will rapidly corrode the metal. A good idea after cleaning metal tools is to rub them over with an oily rag. Hardened plaster on tools can be removed with a wire brush.

Tools for carving plaster
- Stone or wood carving chisels
- Hammer or mallet
- Knives
- Files
- Rasps or Surforms
- Hacksaw blade
- Glasspaper

For mixing plaster
- Bag of plaster
- Water
- Plastic bowls
- Shoe boxes, plastic boxes, etc (to contain plaster while setting to make block)
- Newspaper or sheet of polythene

Technique

There are many ways of making a plaster block for carving. The simplest is to pour the mixed, liquid plaster directly into the shoe box, plastic box or similar container. Long tubular shapes can be made by pouring the plaster into a cardboard cylinder; kitchen rolls, lavatory rolls are suitable. Amorphous shapes can be made by pouring the plaster into a polythene bag, tying up the top and then squeezing it into shape. Other shapes can be made with a wall of clay, or poured into a box of sand. More complicated blocks can be made by casting a number of components, eg from yogurt cups, and cementing them together with large dollops of plaster. The plaster block can be easily removed from any of the moulds mentioned above. Cardboard or clay can be peeled away. Plastic containers allow the plaster block to slide out easily, though sometimes a gentle tap is required to assist the process.

above
Plaster moulds suitable for filling with plaster (shoe box, plastic drain pipe, washing-up liquid container with the top cut off, lavatory roll, yogurt cups, egg box, polythene bag)
left
Plaster shapes cast from some of the moulds mentioned. The hand was cast from a rubber glove

Mixing plaster

In order to make a good, strong block, it is important to observe a few simple rules. Most important is always to add the plaster to the water. The water must be cold. Before starting to mix the plaster, assess how much liquid plaster you require to fill the mould. Then choose a suitably sized mixing container, eg bucket, bowl, etc. As a very rough estimate the total volume that will be required is made up of 50 per cent water and 50 per cent plaster. It is more economical to mix less rather than more plaster than is required. It is always possible to mix a little more but disheartening to be left with half a bucket of liquid plaster and nothing to do with it! A safer way of assessing volumes beforehand is to fill the mould that you intend using with water. Pour the water into the mixing bowl and pour away a little over half. By the time the plaster has been mixed into the water remaining in the bucket there should be about the right amount to fill the mould.

Before mixing the plaster check that the room is well prepared. Searching for a forgotten piece of equipment with hands covered in plaster is best avoided. Cover the bench with a polythene sheet or newspaper. A few sheets of newspaper on the floor helps to prevent the plaster being trodden in. Place the container of plaster away from the source of water so that it remains dry. Take the mixing bowl containing the correct amount of water to the plaster and with a dry hand sprinkle handfuls into the water. Do not mix at this stage. Continue sifting the plaster through the fingers into the water (this method helps to prevent lumps from forming) until the depth of plaster reaches the surface of the water. Leave the mixture in this stage for about half a minute before gently stirring the mixture to a creamy consistency. Do not agitate the plaster briskly or air bubbles will be incorporated into the plaster mix. The mixed plaster should have the consistency of single cream. As soon as the plaster is mixed pour it into the mould and tap the container to remove any pockets of air. The plaster will soon start to thicken and then set hard. Leave the mould undisturbed during this time and for at least an hour before carefully removing the block. During part of this setting time a chemical reaction produces a heat that makes the plaster feel warm.

Sifting the plaster through the fingers and sprinkling it into the water

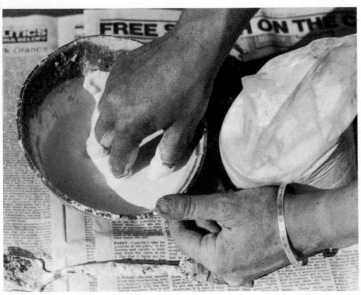

Gently mixing in the plaster

Hands or anything covered in liquid plaster should not be washed in the sink, otherwise it will quickly block. A bowl of water placed on the draining board for washing hands avoids the risk of blocked pipes. Several hours later, when the chemical action of the plaster is over, it is safe to pour off the clean water from the surface and throw away or dry out the sludge to dispose of it.

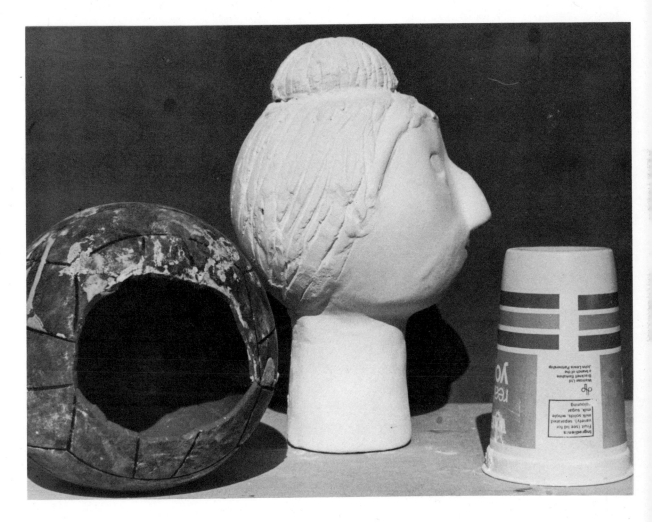

A head made from a football and a large yogurt cup. The neck was cast first by filling the yogurt cup with liquid plaster. When it had set the plaster shape was removed from the yogurt cup. The football had a hole cut in it before being filled with plaster. Before the plaster set the plaster block for the neck was inserted through the hole in the football. When the plaster in the football had set small slits were cut in the rubber to allow the plaster head to be removed. The bun was made by partly filling the yogurt cup with plaster and when set it was stuck to the head with a dollop of plaster. Another dollop was added for the nose. The head was then carved with a knife and finished off with glasspaper when completely dry

108

Plaster blocks cast from large and small yogurt cups being built up into two columns. Freshly mixed plaster is used to stick them together

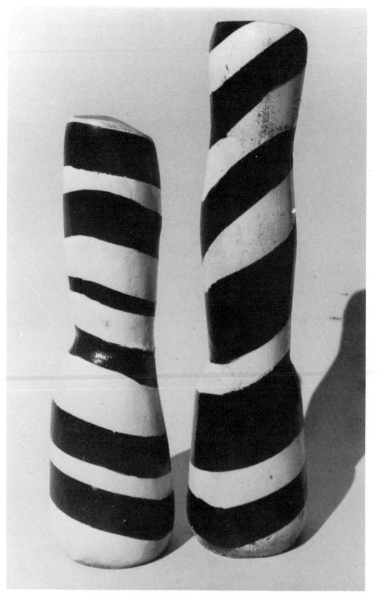

Two columns. The completed columns were shaped with Surform files and left to dry out completely. They were then glasspapered and painted with two coats of varnish to seal the plaster. Finally they were painted black and a design prepared by sticking on masking tape. The exposed areas were painted white and the masking tape pulled off to reveal the black areas

Carving the plaster block
Much of the rough shaping of the block can be done immediately the plaster is removed from the mould. While it is still wet it is at its softest. Carve the plaster carefully, avoiding heavy blows. If the block is small enough to be held in the hand it can be carved with a knife (taking care to cut away from the hands and body). As the plaster dries out it will take more detail. To glasspaper the plaster to a very smooth finish it is necessary to dry it out completely. This can be done by leaving the plaster in a warm dry place such as an airing cupboard or oven for several days.

Surforms *Surform* files are made in a variety of shapes and are invaluable for plaster work. The little cuts in the surface of the file not only bite into the plaster very effectively but also allow the plaster filings to pass through the holes and thus prevent clogging.

Tools for carving plaster
A selection of these are useful: flat *Surform*, round *Surform*, old wood chisels, stone chisels, mallet, knife, small craft knife, metal spatula, plaster tools with serrated edges, broken piece of hacksaw blade, small file, flat piece of metal, small *Surform* plane, broken piece of *Surform* file, glasspaper.

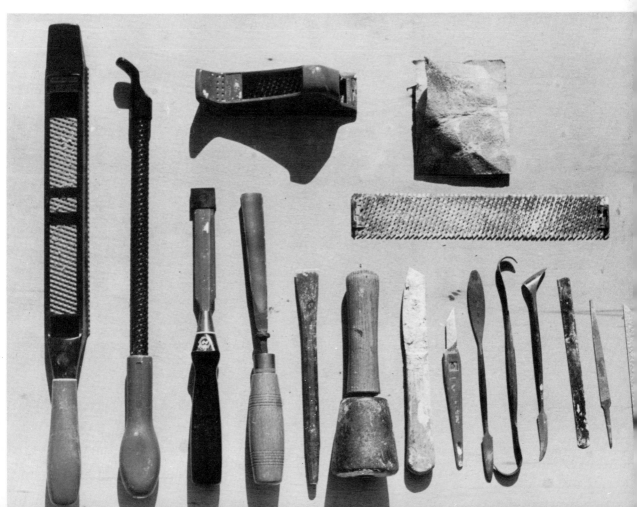

Making a circular plaque

Smear *Vaseline* (soap or oil will do) on the inside of a washing up bowl. This prevents the plaster from sticking if the washing up bowl is rather old. Pour liquid plaster into the bowl to a depth of about 15 mm ($\frac{5}{8}$ in.)

When the plaster has hardened place a piece of chicken wire over it for reinforcement. Pour enough plaster over to cover it completely – about 10 mm ($\frac{3}{8}$ in.)

Before the plaster begins to set, quickly put two screw eyes into the plaster so that only the eye protrudes from the surface of the plaster. The screw eyes can be made more secure by tying a short length of string or wire around each and pushing it into the plaster. This should help to reinforce the screw eye in the plaster and prevent it pulling out

When the plaster has hardened it can be removed from the polythene bowl which was acting as a mould

The design has been drawn onto the plaster with a pencil and then carved with knives or lino tools

Casting and carving a plaster block

A cardboard box was first lined with thin polythene (to prevent leaks). The polythene was secured round the top of the box with sticking tape to prevent the polythene falling into the plaster. A bucket of plaster was mixed and poured into the box

To reinforce the plaster block, pieces of glass fibre matting were cut (hessian, burlap, or sacking with an open weave will do). Glass fibre is used as reinforcement with plastic resins in the manufacture of fibreglass products. It can be obtained either as offcuts from manufacturers, or from sculpture suppliers

An iron rod was put in the box with one end protruding through a hole made in the side of the box. (This is so that it can later be set in a plaster base). The strips of glass fibre matting were then dipped in liquid plaster and laid over the iron rod to provide strong reinforcement. Another bucketful of plaster was mixed and the cardboard box filled almost to the top. When the plaster has set the cardboard box can be peeled away from the block

The plaster block has been removed from the mould. The iron rod can be seen protruding from the block

Block set in plaster base. This was done by holding the plaster block upright in a small cardboard box. Plaster was then poured in to a depth that covered the iron bar and part of the block itself. Pieces of chicken wire were pushed below the surface of the liquid plaster to reinforce it. When the plaster had set the cardboard box was peeled away

Carving the plaster block with a hammer and chisel

Filing the sculpture using a *Surform* file

Completed carving. *Two Women* by Edwin
Beecroft

Finishes

Colour may be added as part of the plaster mix
or as a superficial treatment of the surface.

Integral colour treatment Any colour applied
to plaster must be lime free. Earth colours and
metallic oxides are most suitable. The best
method is to spoon some powder colour onto a
square of fine muslin and tie it tightly. This can
then be dipped in to the mixing water (like a
blue bag), before the plaster is added, until the
desired colour is reached. Remember that with
the addition of white plaster the colour will be
considerably lightened. This method avoids the
streakiness that occurs when the paint is added
to the liquid, mixed plaster. An alternative
method is to mix powder colour thoroughly
with dry plaster before adding it to the water.
The advantage of adding colour as an integral
part is that scratches and chips do not show as
much.

Superficial colour treatment Substances used
for surface colouring of plaster include oil
paint, emulsion, tempera, metallic finishes, and
resins.
   The usual way of applying colour to the
surface of plaster is first to give it several coats
of diluted PVA glue, shellac dissolved in
alcohol, or polyurethane varnish. The plaster
must be perfectly dry. Each coat applied must
be allowed time to dry completely before the
next is applied. In the case of polyurethane
varnish it is necessary to rub it over lightly with
very fine glasspaper between coats and before
applying the colour.
   Milk can be used to change the external
surface of plaster. Repeated saturation of
sculpture in milk, with thorough drying out
between each application, will make a marble-
like effect. Another method is to add skimmed
milk to the mixing water before the addition of
powdered plaster. This allows the plaster to be
polished when dry.
   If oil colour is to be applied the plaster
should be thoroughly soaked in linseed oil. The
oil colour may then be painted on directly.
When dry the surface should be rubbed lightly
with silk. The oil colour can be applied using
any consistency. Varying degrees of
transparency can be achieved depending on the

amount of turpentine used to dilute the oil colour.

Uniform coloured effects can be achieved with aerosol paint sprays, car paint sprays or any household paint. The plaster should first be primed with a paint primer, shellac or varnish, using several coats painted directly onto the dry plaster surface.

In order to preserve the whiteness of plaster several coats of a durable, washable emulsion will seal the surface effectively. Alternatively, the plaster can be treated with several coats of clear varnish.

Bronzing   This process gives plaster sculpture a simulated bronze effect. Plaster surfaces should be free from moisture and sealed with shellac.

Small pots of powder are sold in a variety of metal colours such as medium bronze, copper, silver bronze etc. They also sell a selection of earth colours. The small pots of metal powder seem expensive but where a metallic finish is required this will give the most realistic effect. Used sparingly, the powders will last for a surprisingly long time.

To apply the metal powder, each colour needs to be mixed with a small amount of shellac and painted on with a soft brush. Sometimes more than one coat is necessary. A technique often used is to coat the sculpture with a dark earth colour, eg raw umber, then to paint on a medium bronze and copper mixture, leaving a little of the umber showing in the deepest hollows. Finally, a light bronze is applied to the projecting parts to highlight them. To remove any garish quality, a tin of graphite is useful. This can be applied in small quantities with the bronze powder. Graphite is a useful powder. It is quite cheap and can be used on its own with shellac to create lead coloured effects on plaster.

Metallic finishes   There are tubes of a metallic coloured cream that can be rubbed on a surface to give a simulated metal effect, and then buffed to a shine. *Goldfinger* and *Rub and Buff* are two of the trade names. They can be bought in a number of different metal colours and are sold in most art shops. The plaster should first be sealed with several coats of shellac before applying the paste.

Durable finishes   More durable finishes can be achieved by painting the surface with polyester resin containing a colour pigment and hardener. The use of polyester resins is a specialized subject and they should only be used where there is a sound knowledge of their properties and application. There are other resins on the market, sold in packs with comprehensive instructions. An excellent product of this type is *Devcon*.

Devcon is a metallic epoxy resin that can be painted over plaster to give a durable surface with a glossy metal coloured finish. Plaster should first be sealed with a coat of polyurethane varnish. This product is sold in different coloured metals such as bronze, aluminium, steel and lead. The packs contain the plastic metal, hardening agent, release agent (not required for use as a surface finish), measuring spoons and complete instructions. The plastic metal contains a high amount of metal (about 80 per cent) and a small amount of epoxy resin (about 20 per cent), which gives a fairly realistic effect. When the plastic metal has hardened the gloss can be removed and highlighting effects achieved by rubbing with steel wool.

Electro-plating is a process by which a plaster surface can be given a thin coating of metal. The price varies according to the size of the sculpture and type of metal chosen. Gold is obviously the most expensive, silver somewhat cheaper, and brass and copper cheapest of all. A small sculpture electro-plated in copper can be done for quite a reasonable price. The advantage of this is that the sculpture is given a thin covering of real metal which makes the plaster more durable and gives the sculpture the appearance of being made of metal. Addresses of electro-platers can be found in the Yellow Pages of the telephone directory.

Other plaster-based products

Polyfilla

Polyfilla is a plaster based cellulose compound used for do-it-yourself repairs such as filling holes and cracks in walls. Its use as a sculpture medium has increased greatly in the last few years. This is probably as the result of a national competition that Polycell Products Ltd have run for several years in schools. *Polyfilla* makes a good material to cast into a block and carve. It is readily cut and sanded and has good resilience and resistance to carving. Where corrections need to be made to the sculpture, it is easy to add on some more and re-work the area. *Polyfilla* is more often used for small sculpture, as it is more expensive than plaster. However, *Polyfilla* has the advantage of being easily obtainable, supplied in neat packaging, and is cleaner to work with than plaster.

Obtaining Polyfilla   *Polyfilla* is one of the *Polycell* range of products. It is available from do-it-yourself shops everywhere.

Tools and equipment, approach and finishes, are all identical to working with plaster.

Plastic stone

Stolit is the name of a plastic stone designed for manufacturing industrial castings such as pattern plates. *Stolit* is not a widely known material for sculpture. Its potential was first recognised by sculptors such as Lynn Chadwick in the fifties. *Stolit* can be used in exactly the same way as plaster and although expensive it offers more durable and permanent qualities.

Stolit is often described as a plastic stone, though it may also be known as artificial stone or composition. It is available in two colours, red and white. Both colours take on a mellow quality when mixed with water and allowed time to set hard. The white powder becomes grey when mixed with water but after setting it dries to a rust colour which some sculptors alter to greens and blacks with the application of acids. The red powder dries to a terracotta colour. *Stolit* is much harder to carve than plaster.

Obtaining Stolit   *Stolit* is sold in drums of 50 kilos (1 cwt) by the manufacturer, the White Sea and Baltic Company, (F and M Supplies Division), Patman House, George Lane, South Woodford, London E18.

Chessmen. These were made by casting cylinders of *Polyfilla* from cardboard kitchen roll tubes. The *Polyfilla* cylinders were then cut up to the correct lengths for the different chessmen and filed to shape using Surforms. (The round Surform was particularly useful)

Reclining Figure by Edwin Beecroft. A thick covering of *Stolit* was built up over a frame of expanded metal (chicken wire will do). This metal frame should be stuffed with newspaper to prevent the *Stolit* falling through the holes. The sculpture was carved using knives, rasps and files. The finished sculpture was left to dry before being given several applications of wax polish

Ring of Children carved from *Stolit*. The round block for carving was made by filling a plastic cup with *Stolit* and holding a piece of clay in the centre until the *Stolit* had set. This made the block a cup-like shape. The separation of the figures was made by drilling small holes. The detail was made with the use of small knives and files

Building blocks

Autoclaved aerated concrete building blocks –
to give them their full name – are widely used in
the building industry. Introduced into England
in the 1950s, they are a relatively new sculpture
material.

Building blocks are manufactured from
finely ground sand, lime and cement. These
materials are mixed to a slurry by the addition
of water. A trace of aluminium powder is then
mixed with the slurry which causes a reaction
that produces hydrogen gas. This expands the
volume of the slurry which produces the
cellular structure of the material. It is this
cellular structure that makes the material so
easy to carve.

The carving of autoclaved aerated concrete
blocks has been common in Sweden for many
years. In English schools their advantages are
now becoming recognised. Their main feature
is that they are light to handle and easy to carve
while also being a substantial and satisfying
carving medium. Blocks are cheap, readily
obtainable and can be carved without
sophisticated tools and equipment. The one
drawback is the dust that is made when they
are carved. Wherever possible they should be
carved out of doors. It is a wise precaution to
wear a mask or scarf covering the nose and
mouth to prevent inhaling the dust.

A range of autoclaved aerated concrete
building blocks (Courtesy Durox Building
Units Ltd)

Obtaining building blocks
Building blocks can be bought in a variety of
sizes and thicknesses from most builders'
merchants. Where blocks are unobtainable
locally enquiries should be made to either of
the firms listed on page 138.

Tools and equipment
Bench or strong table
Stone or woodcarving chisels (preferably old
ones)
Sharpening stone (tools blunt quickly in
contact with building blocks)
A selection of the following are useful:
Saws
Hacksaw blade
Knives
Files   } these can be used
Rasps   instead of chisels
Surforms
Spoons

Tools for carving building blocks

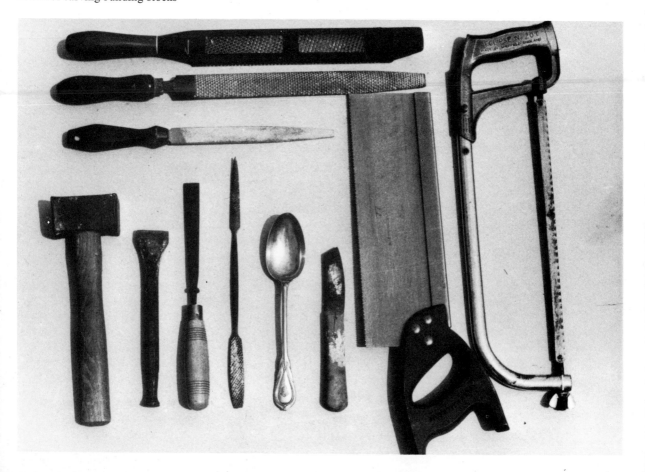

Technique

The porous quality of the building blocks makes it necessary to carve broad, bold sculpture. Details and sharp projections should be avoided. Holes can be bored or drilled through the block. Several blocks can be joined with a short piece of dowelling inserted between each block and glued into place. Sculpture can also be constructed from blocks cut to form interlocking parts. Mortar can be used to join blocks together. A suitable mortar would be 1 part of masonry cement to 4 parts of sand. The blocks should be well dampened prior to bonding, and the joints should be about 10 mm ($\frac{3}{8}$ in) thick. Where thinner joints are required *Durox* suggest their proprietary product *Durojoin*. This is a dry packed blend of specially graded sand, cement and certain bond improving additives. It can be used to produce joints of 2–5 mm ($\frac{1}{16}$–$\frac{3}{16}$ in) thickness.

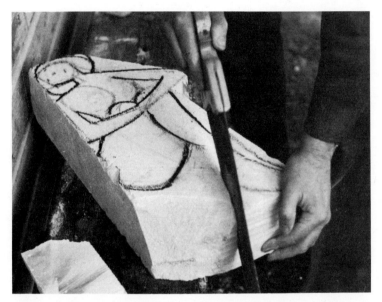

The design should be drawn onto the block with charcoal. Large unwanted areas may then be removed with a saw. This takes some of the hard work out of the preliminary carving

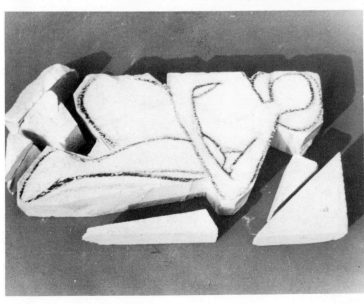

Pieces removed from the block. (It is worth keeping the larger pieces as these can also be used for carving)

Drilling through the block to make the carving of holes easier. As the depth of the block was greater than that of the drill bit, it was necessary to drill holes from each side

Shaping the sculpture using a Surform file

The Magi by William Mitchell. This sculpture is carved from a large number of blocks that have been joined together. The sculpture was carved using an industrial technique called sand blasting (Courtesy Thermalite Ltd)

Finishes

The rough quality of building blocks is not easily altered. It is best to consider this rough texture as part of the sculpture from the beginning. Glasspapering will give a slightly smoother, more finished appearance. The surface may be stained or painted. Paint can be applied with a brush or from an aerosol spray. Several coats are necessary to cover the porous surface of the block. Sculpture carved from building blocks is suitable for outdoor conditions.

Weeping Lady by J. Mound (Courtesy Thermalite Ltd)

Shapes 8 and 9 by Iain Anderson

Brick

The use of brick as an artistic medium is an ancient one. There are examples of brick sculpture dating back to 1590 BC. In England brick was not introduced until the sixteenth century and it has continued to be used as a decorative medium until the last two decades, when it rather declined in popularity. More recently there has been a degree of renewed interest in brick carving and commissioned works have been executed by sculptors such as Walter Ritchie. Brick has many features to recommend it as a sculptural medium. It is certainly an ideal medium for outdoor sculpture. Examples of carved brickwork exist that have survived two hundred years of exposure to weather conditions with no noticeable effect. Brick can be carved in the form of large-scale reliefs or decorative wall panels. A wall panel can be built up in brick and specifically designed for the carving. Alternatively, a relief sculpture can be carved from any existing wall, provided the brick is of even texture. Sculptures can also be carved from individual bricks. When carving a relief from an existing brick wall, one occasionally finds a brick that fractures as a result of it having been overfired. The fractured brick can be cut out and replaced without too much difficulty. Brick walls that have not been purpose-made for carving may have weaknesses through the bricks being laid too dry. The impact of carving may shake the mortar loose in some places. These areas can be repaired by mixing some mortar, damping the surrounding brickwork and pushing the freshly mixed mortar into the gaps. Make sure before repairing the holes that all the loose particles have been brushed away.

Bricks, individually, are fairly fragile so it is important when carving a single brick to avoid heavy blows with the hammer. Carving should be executed with care, removing small pieces at a time. The porous composition of bricks means that sharp projections should be avoided. Soft flowing shapes are far more suitable to the medium.

Types of brick

Clay bricks   Ordinary house bricks can be used for carving. Most of the red clay variety are suitable although it is wise to test them first by breaking one in half to check that it has an even texture without too many flaws, such as shrinkage cracks. Old bricks can often be found on demolition sites or around derelict buildings. Inspect the bricks first for frost damage. If they have fracture lines or crumble when handled they are too damaged to carve. New bricks can be bought from builders merchants.

Sand lime bricks   Sand lime bricks have a different feel to clay bricks. They are made from different materials and by a different process from traditional clay bricks. This results in a denser, slightly granular feel to the brick. The lime in the brick gives them a natural white colour but most brickmakers also sell a coloured range of the same brick. Sand lime bricks are quite soft and fairly easy to carve. This type of brick is stocked by most builders merchants. When buying bricks check that the colour goes all the way through. Some bricks are made with the colour on the outside only.

Tools and equipment
 Bench or strong table
 Vice or G-cramp
 Hammer and stone carving chisels
 Sharpening stone (an old piece of paving stone will do)
 Rasp and file
 Glasspaper

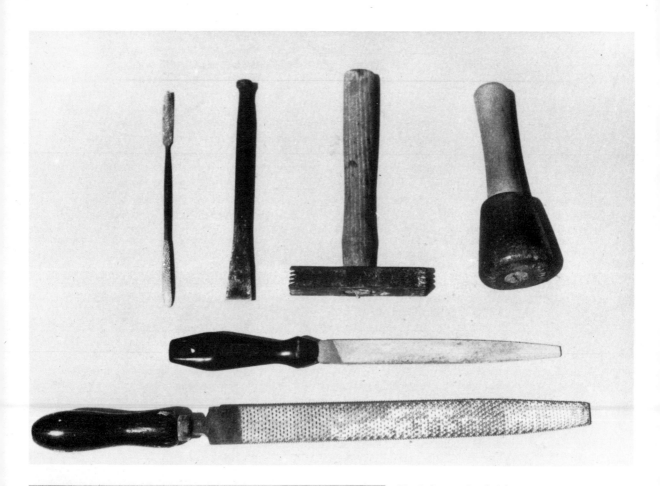

Tools for carving brick

Technique

Grey sand lime bricks and an old red house brick. These old bricks often have a soft weathered texture that makes them very easy to carve

Removing the corners and edges with a hammer and chisel. After this initial stage the brick must be shaped, removing small pieces at a time to avoid the risk of the brick fracturing

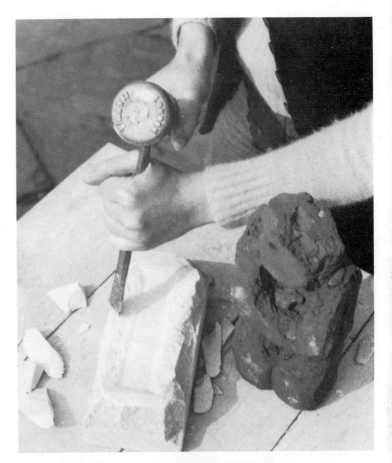

When the sculpture has been chiselled to shape, the surfaces can be smoothed with a rasp, file and glasspaper

128

Abrasive attachments on an electric drill can be useful for smoothing surfaces. Brick is a very dusty material to work, even with hand tools. When sanding with an electric drill protective clothing – goggles, mask or scarf, and an overall – are essential

The sculptor Walter Ritchie carving a relief panel in red facing brick. The design has been drawn onto the brickwork in chalk (Courtesy The Brick Development Association)

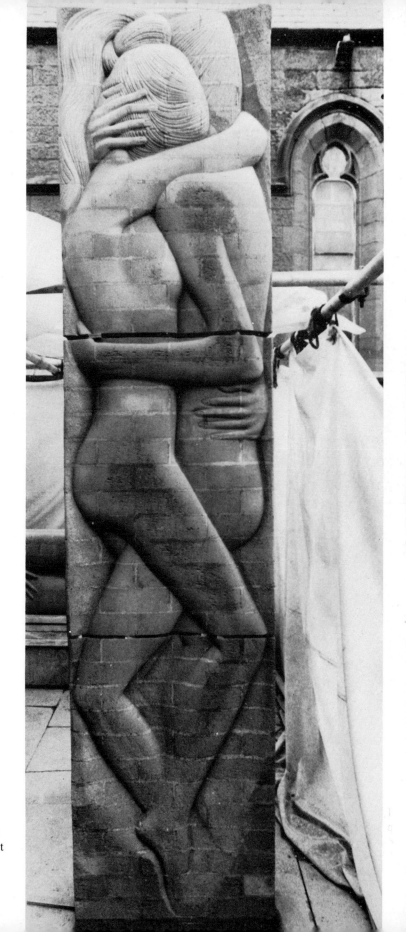

The finished panel. *Takes Herrick's advice.*
This is from a sequence of large brick panels
depicting episodes in the 'adventurous life' of
the entirely mythical Lady Sarah Wellington-
Gore. Walter Richie was commissioned to
produce this series by The Brick Development
Association (Courtesy The Brick Development
Association)

130

Detail of *The Lady plays with her kittens*, part
of the same series by Walter Ritchie (Courtesy
The Brick Development Association)

Acrylic plastic

Acrylic plastic is one of the most attractive of the man-made materials. Its translucent quality transmits light which adds an unusual and exciting quality to sculpture. Apart from glass there are few materials that allow the light both to filter through and to flow over the form. It can be polished to a highly reflective finish. Acrylic plastic is available in a wide range of colours, and comes in translucent, transparent, opaque or opal finishes. It can be bought as sheets, rods, or blocks, all of which are suitable for sculpture purposes. In a country where plastic has become so much a part of our lives it is an interesting exercise to try working in one of the most recent materials to sculpture. Some sculptors have balked at the idea of working in plastic and consider that traditional materials are more suitable. For others, acrylic plastic has provided stimulating and exciting qualities offering a new set of aesthetic problems and a new approach to sculpture.

There are certain technical problems to master when using acrylic. It is a tough and brittle material which can be carved with wood carving tools and which can also be sawn and abraded. It is quite difficult to carve and certainly requires some persistence. Sculptors who have mastered the technique have achieved some interesting and worthwhile results. The use of power drills makes the process of carving far easier but it is certainly not a very suitable carving medium for children.

Obtaining acrylic

Acrylic is one of the most expensive of the man-made materials suitable for carving. It is worthwhile trying to buy offcuts which are much cheaper. Likely firms to try for offcuts are sign makers and manufacturers of goods in acrylic. Addresses can usually be found in the Yellow Pages of the telephone directory under the heading 'Plastics'. The references to look out for are acrylic, *Perspex* and *Plexiglas*. Other types of plastic listed as plastic resin or plastic sheeting are unsuitable. Where there is difficulty in obtaining acrylic it can be bought from the firms listed in the suppliers, although these firms generally only handle fairly large orders.

Tools and equipment

Bench or table
Vice or G-cramp
Hacksaw or tenon saw
Wood chisels (not essential)
Files and Surforms
Electric drill and sanding attachments
Wet and dry silicon carbide abrasive paper
Metal polish or jeweller's rouge

Some of the tools that are useful for carving acrylic: felt tip pen (for drawing design onto the acrylic), hacksaw, wood mallet, dummy mallet, wood chisels, files, Surform and tenon saw

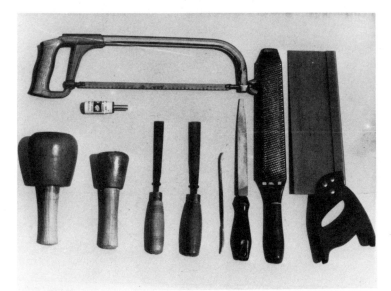

Block of acrylic plastic

Design for sculpture drawn onto the block with felt tip pen. The parts to be cut away have been blacked out

Unwanted areas of the sculpture have been removed with a saw. This takes some of the hard work out of carving. (In the case of this particular block its thickness made it rather hard to saw by hand so it was taken to a firm with an electric band saw). The sculpture was then carved with wood chisels. It is most important to wear protective goggles or glasses as flying chips of acrylic are extremely sharp. It is not necessary to use wood chisels. The sculpture can be planned so that all the large areas are sawn away and the shaping is done with rasps, files or an electric drill with sanding attachments

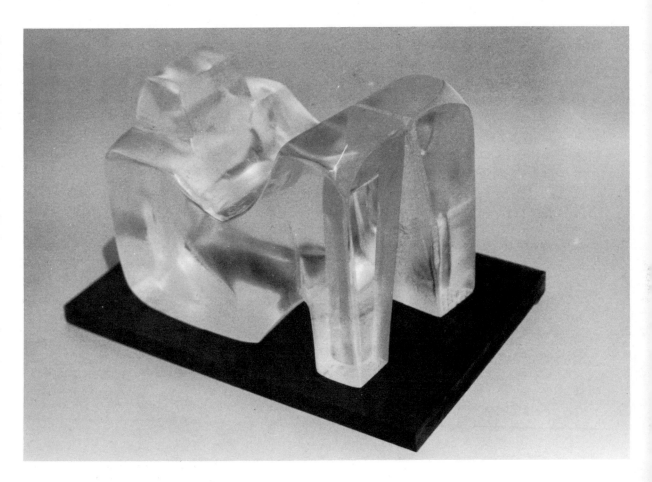

The completed sculpture. Achieving a fine
polished surface on the acrylic is very slow
work. Buy as many grades of wet and dry
paper as you can and be prepared for a lot of
rubbing. The best way to work is to select the
coarsest grade of wet and dry and to rub the
whole surface of the sculpture, a small area at a
time, in a circular motion. When the whole
surface appears smooth progress to the next
grade of abrasive paper until you have reached
the finest grade. Always use the abrasive paper
with water so that a creamy paste is made as
the surface of the acrylic is abraded. Finally a
polished finish can be achieved with metal
polish or jewellers rouge applied with a rag.
Alternatively, a buffing polish applied to a
polishing mop on an electric drill will
effectively polish acrylic plastic

134

Marcel Ronay, sculptor and engraver with one
of his sculptures carved from a block of
Perspex (Courtesy ICI)

Cutting

Acrylic can be cut using a hacksaw or a fine toothed tenon saw but care must be taken not to splinter the material by too vigorous use of the saw. Sawing acrylic by hand is slow and laborious so only fairly small jobs should be attempted. Where available an electric circular saw or bandsaw will cut through acrylic easily. It is important to feed the material slowly and steadily to the saw to avoid the build up of excessive heat during cutting.

Cementing

Pieces of acrylic plastic can be joined together with the use of an appropriate cement. Manufacturers of acrylic materials are generally able to advise on suitable cements for their products, and most adhesive manufacturers state the materials for which their particular adhesives are suitable. ICI Plastics Division manufactures a range of *Tensol* cements that can be bought from most suppliers of *Perspex*.

When joining acrylic with cement it is essential that surfaces to be joined should be properly prepared in order to achieve maximum bond strength. Surfaces should be clean, dry and free from grease. Items to be cemented can be washed in warm (50°–60°C) (106°–140°F) water which contains a small amount of liquid detergent and then rinsed with clear warm water and allowed to dry. Highly polished surfaces should be roughened with glasspaper or emery cloth in order to encourage the cement to wet the surface more thoroughly. Surfaces stuck with an acrylic cement will form a far stronger bond than if stuck with an adhesive such as *Araldite*. This is because the chemical reaction of the cement with the acrylic causes the surfaces to fuse.

Cutting, filing and polishing acrylic plastic will produce some internal stress in the material. Unless removed by annealing at 87°–93°C (188°–199°F) this stress will cause the surface to craze when acrylic cement is applied. This crazing effect can sometimes be attractive but if it is not wanted, it can be prevented by following the instructions given in the Appendix, page 137.

Sheet acrylic

Sheets of acrylic are sold with a protective sheet of paper stuck to them. This is useful for drawing the shapes onto the acrylic sheet before cutting them out. The approach to working with sheets of acrylic is simpler than carving blocks. The shapes can be more easily cut out with a fine tenon or hacksaw. The backing paper can then be peeled off and the edges of the cut shapes cleaned with wet and dry paper.

Local bending of acrylic sheet   Simple bends may be made in acrylic sheet by the application of heat. To bend a piece of sheet, first make a small mark with a wax pencil at each end of the line along which the bend is to be made.

Acrylic sheet can conveniently be heated in an electric oven for shaping. The oven should be capable of being controlled at temperatures between 120°C and 170°C (248°–338°F). It is advisable to cover the shelves with brown paper or to place the cut shapes on baking sheets, to minimise damage to the surface of the sheet. Plastic materials are poor conductors of heat, thus adequate time must be allowed for the centre of the sheet to reach the required temperature. Acrylic sheet can be shaped at a temperature of 160°–170°C (320°–338°F) but will suffer surface damage if heated to temperatures much in excess of 180°C (356°F). It is therefore necessary to set the oven to a maximum of 170°C (338°F) and allow time for the sheet to be heated throughout, which in practice requires about 20 minutes for 3 mm ($\frac{1}{8}$ in) sheet, 30 minutes for 6 mm ($\frac{1}{4}$ in) sheet. Provided that the oven temperature is adequately controlled it is better to leave the sheet in the oven for longer than necessary rather than try to shape it before it is evenly heated. It is of interest that acrylic sheet that has been shaped by the application of heat will revert to a flat sheet if it is reheated to its shaping temperature, unless it has been damaged during the shaping. This means that unsuccessful shapings can often be recovered for further use.

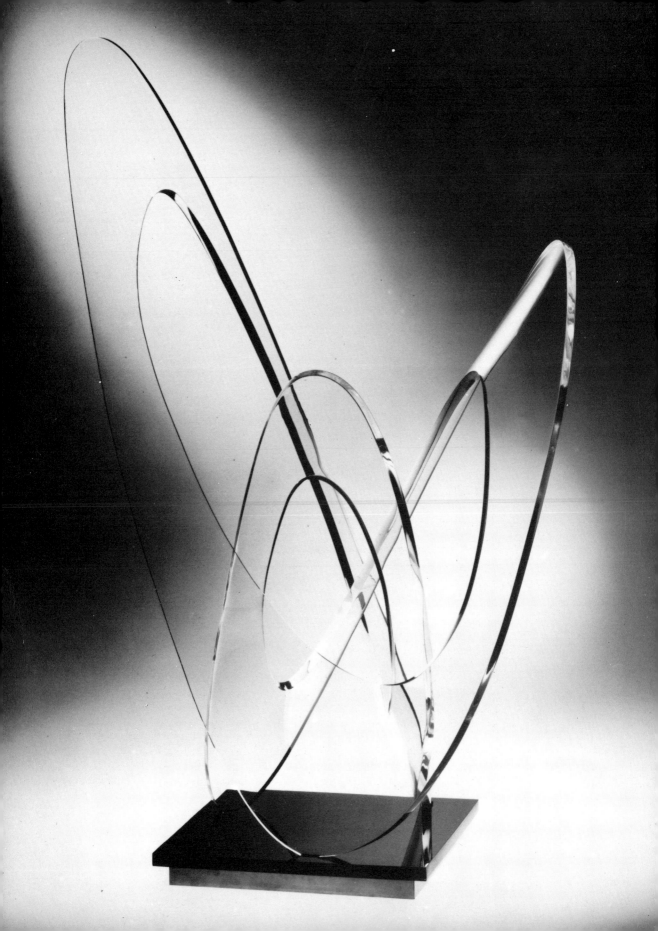

Appendix

Annealing

The following instructions for annealing acrylic plastic are taken from the ICI publication *'Perspex' acrylic sheet. Technical Service note PX119.*

Because it is possible to introduce both thermal and mechanical strains into the material during machining processes, it may be found that crazing develops after a period varying from a few hours to several months. It is therefore necessary to carry out an annealing cycle after machining to guard against such long-term effects, and in some instances, when a succession of machining operations is required, it may also be necessary to introduce an inter-stage annealing cycle.

Annealing is carried out by slowly heating the machined part up to a temperature in the range 87°–93°C (189°–199°F), maintaining it at that temperature for a time, and then slowly cooling it so as to avoid the risk of reintroducing thermal strains. In the following formulae:

T = time in hours
y = sheet thickness in millimetres

(i) Load the oven and raise to annealing temperature at a rate not exceeding 18°C (32°F) per hour

(ii) Holding time at

87°–93°C (189°–199°F); $T = \dfrac{y}{3}$

(iii) Cooling time to room temperature. (A cooling rate of 12°C (22°F) per hour should be used if this gives a longer time than that obtained from the calculation);

$T = \dfrac{y}{4}$

If any section of a component has been heat-formed it will be necessary to restrict the annealing temperature to 70°–85°C (158°–185°F), the precise temperature depending upon the degree of stretch in the heat-formed part.

Highly stretched heat-formed components should be limited to a temperature of 70°C (158°F) and the cycle times, (i), (ii), and (iii) all extended by 25 per cent.

Winged Victory by Leslie Summers. This sculpture is made in *Perspex* acrylic sheet, manufactured by ICI (Courtesy ICI)

Suppliers in Great Britain

General
Alec Tiranti Limited
21 Goodge Place, London W1 and
70 High Street, Theale, Berkshire

Salt
Many small grocers and delicatessen shops
Enquiries as to nearest local stockist from
Ingram and Sons Limited
Lion Salt Works, Narston,
nr Northwich, Cheshire

Glycerine soap
Saddlers or shops selling leather goods

Balsa wood
Leading suppliers of art materials
Balsa Imports Limited
38 Bow Lane, Cannon Street, London EC4

Packs from
E J Arnold and Son Limited (School Suppliers)
Butterley Street, Leeds, Yorkshire

Clay
Fulham Pottery Limited
210 New Kings Road, London SW6

W Podmore and Sons Limited
Caledonian Mills, Shelton, Stoke on Trent

Wax
Candle making kits and blocks of wax from
Candle Makers Supplies
4 Beaconsfield Terrace Road,
London W14 0PP

Paraffin wax
Stocked by most large chemists

Expanded polystyrene and polyurethane
The Baxenden Chemical Co Limited
Paragon Works, Baxenden, Accrington,
Lancashire

Alostone, Formablock, Das, Barbola Paste, Newclay, Instant Wood
E J Arnold and Son Limited (School Suppliers)
Butterley Street, Leeds, Yorkshire

Stone and chalk
Shearman and Co Limited
Vicarage Road, Abbotskerswell, Newton Abbot, Devon

York stone (for sharpening stone carving chisels)
Most builders' merchants or suppliers
of garden stone

Wood
Fitchett and Woolacott
Popham Street, off Canal Walk, Nottingham

Plaster of paris
Builders' merchants
Boots Chemists (dental plaster)
Gyproc Limited, Ferguson House, Marylebone
Road, London NW1

Polyfilla
Do-It-Yourself shops, department stores,
hardware stores

Stolit
The White Sea and Baltic Company
(F and M Supplies Division)
Patmore House, George Lane
South Woodford, London E18

Building blocks
Thermalite Limited
Hams Hall, Lea Marston, Sutton Coldfield,
Warwickshire

Durox Building Units Limited
Northumberland Road, Linford,
nr Stanford le Hope, Essex

Bricks
Builders' merchants

Acrylic plastic
ICI Plastics Division
Welwyn Garden City, Hertfordshire

G H Bloore Limited
Honeypot Lane, Stanmore, Middlesex

Suppliers in the USA

Mail-order catalogs obtainable on request from:

Art Brown and Brothers Inc
2 West 46 Street
New York, NY 10036
*also supply metal modeling compound
(aluminium and bronze) minimum order $20 and
self-hardening clays*

Sculpture Associates Ltd
114 East 25 Street
New York, NY 10010

Sculpture House
38 East 30 Street
New York, NY 10016

Sculpture Services Inc
9 East 19 Street
New York, NY 10003

Goldfinger, Rub and Buff
Leisure Craft Limited
3061 East Maria Street
Compton, California

Metal modeling compound
Should be available in art supply stores that
carry sculpture materials

Self-hardening clays
From any art supply store that carries
sculpture supplies.

There is also a product called *Sculpey* which
stays soft until baked in an ordinary oven.
Once baked, *Sculpey* can be carved, sanded,
and painted. There is also *Celluclay*, a
powdered form of papier mâché which can be
cut, sanded, and painted when dry. Obtainable
through Art Brown and Brothers Inc.

Index